What's Cooking?...

everyone is busy...

THESE DAYS IT SEEMS, EVERYONE IS BUSY. LIFE ON THE RUN HAS COME

to mean eating on the run. Gone are the days of having all day to prepare a meal,

in fact in preference to the purgatory idea of cooking at home, many people prefer

to opt for a quick fix diet a la local D E L I, fast food joint or corner cafe.

Unless you are well organised, it's very easy to find yourself at the end

of a day without having eaten at all, or feeling guilty because you had to resort

to the L O C A L restaurant again, or feeling queasy because you loaded up

on fatty takeaways. Turning the corner cafe into your daily dining room is a

luxury few can afford, and making fast food a regular event is something neither

your health or pocket will thank you for.

The purpose of this book is to show you just how E A S Y it is to eat

well at home, in spite of a busy lifestyle. Whether you're single, living as a couple

or doing the full family bit, there's something here for you.

While there are a number of recipes that require actual cooking, the

E M P H A S I S with this book is more on choosing and assembling

combinations of ingredients. The preparation involved doesn't assume a high

level of culinary knowledge or skill, but the R E S U L T S will be enjoyed by

cooks and non-cooks alike.

I hope this book will show that interesting, inexpensive food isn't an

impossible dream. You just need to know the right tricks.

Enjoy

Annabel Langbein

4

Setting up

WHEN YOU'RE TIRED AND HUNGRY, IT'S VIRTUALLY IMPOSSIBLE TO *feel creative. You really just want to eat* IMMEDIATELY, *without having to think too hard. The result is that you end up making the same old things day in, day out. Your culinary style can become dull and predictable.*

Today's well-travelled palates don't want to sit down each night to a traditional plate of sliced meat with three vegetables (apart from the odd spot of COMFORT-FARE, *like mum used to make). Instead, turn more or less the same ingredients into a spicy steak and vegetable sandwich, or a Mexican bread pocket with salad and avocado, and eating at home suddenly becomes* EXCITING. *By changing the way you use ingredients, you can add a fresh twist to everyday fare – and it only takes a little effort.*

Cooking INTERESTING FOOD *does not require a lot of fancy equipment. Glance behind the scenes in any cafe and you'll see there's not much in the way of high-tech gear, let alone space. Cafes don't generally employ the expensive skills of trained chefs, yet they are masters in presenting* STYLISH *fast food. How do they do it? Rest assured there's no 5-star culinary magician behind the scenes.*

By using the freshest quality ingredients, ORGANISING *a well-equipped store cupboard, and putting some time aside to prepare a few things in* ADVANCE, *you'll be able to create attractive, nutritious meals with very little effort. Apart from baking recipes, which require exact measurements to be successful, the proportions of ingredients can be* VARIED *to suit individual palates. I have opted for the middle ground with seasonings, but would suggest you taste everything as you go, and adjust the heat or spice to suit.*

Cook's lesson #1–Go for the Blade

Good knives are the cook's greatest ally. A sharp knife with good balance makes fast work of menial tasks. Invest in a quality knives – a 20-25cm chef's knife, a thin-bladed filleting knife and a paring knife. Store on a wall magnet or in a knife block where they won't get knocked and lose their edge. Have them sharpened regularly.

Cook's lesson #2 – Thin Bottoms Burn

They also pit and buckle, which makes it impossible to cook anything evenly. Remove nasty thin-bottomed pots and pans from your kitchen forever – give them to your children, or your friends' children, for play cooking, or use them in the garden. Heavy pots take longer to heat, but carry their heat evenly. Feel the weight of a pot before buying. Set up with battery of 1 large pot, 1 wok, 1-2 medium pots, a heavy cast-iron frypan that can double as an oven dish, and a small chef's omelette pan (very cheap, available from chefs' equipment stores).

Cook's lesson #3 – Fire up the Heat

When you want to eat quickly, your heat sources need to deliver intense, fast heat. Gas gives you the quickest heat and greater control for stovetop cooking, and a fan-forced oven heats up more quickly and cooks food more evenly than a conventional oven. Microwaves are useful tools, but you will seldom use most of their added gizmos. A 650-watt microwave oven with variable power settings is all you need to defrost and cook.

Cook's Lesson #4–Gearing up

If you can't afford to buy one for yourself, ask your lover, mother, mother-in-law for a food processor. You'll use it all the time. Get a set of mixing/storage bowls, a thin bladed metal slice or spatula (most of them have a thick edge, which is useless) wooden spoons, sieve, grater, lemon zester and chopping board.

Measures – 1 standard cup equals 250ml, 1 tsp equals 5ml, 1 tbsp equals 15ml. Unless otherwise specified microwaved food is cooked at 100% power. Times given are for a 650 watt microwave oven.

b r e a k f a s t

NASTY SURPRISES ARE NEVER WELCOME AT BREAKFAST.

When you're finding the strength to face the day, you don't want to be confronted with a demanding morning meal. Save the gluey rice and Coke for your next trip to Bali.

If you're one of those people who relies solely on a kick-start of CAFFEINE, *then you're missing out badly. Research has shown that people who eat a sustaining breakfast seem to think better and maintain a better performance.*

For midweek dine-and-dash breakfasts, fast, healthy food is the order of the day. Keep a stock of interesting MUESLI *and cereals, fruits, tomatoes and avocados. Don't miss out on your fibre fix –* FRESH, *not processed, orange juice delivers the goods, as well as kiwifruit, feijoas and tamarillos.*

Blender drinks are a great option. Whizz chilled milk with a few ice-cubes, and blend in banana, honey and yoghurt. POWER *it up with extra fruit, wheatgerm, brewer's yeast or, dare I say it, green spirulina.*

And what about weekends? They're the time to invite a few friends around for a casual nosh – splendid fresh fruit salad, followed by french toast and lots of hot coffee.

Brunch

Rockmelon and

Raspberries

page 13

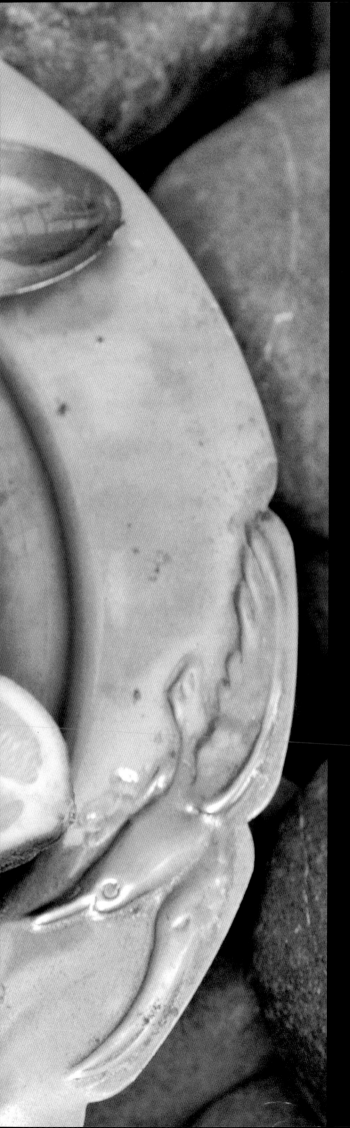

breakfast and brunch...

Fresh Fruit Salad Cup with Greek-Style Yoghurt

Yellow and orange fruits tend to be highest in beta carotene. Half a rockmelon supplies enough vitamin A for the day. A single orange fills your daily requirement for vitamin C, as does 100g strawberries or half a kiwifruit. As vitamin C is destroyed by exposure to oxygen, remove caps from strawberries just before serving and avoid slicing fruits finely.

Prep time: 10 minutes

1kg assorted fresh seasonal fruits (at least 4 different varieties)

1/4 cup passionfruit pulp

2 tbsp runny honey

1/2 cup orange juice

GARNISH – wedges of fresh lime

Break or cut fruit into segments or pieces and remove skins and seeds where necessary.

Combine passionfruit pulp, honey and orange juice. Pour over fruit. Leave for at least 1 hour before serving. Serve lightly chilled with Greek-style yoghurt or whipped cream and lime wedges.

Garnish glasses if desired by dipping the rims in lemon juice or water, then into sugar.

Serves 4-6.

Greek-Style Yoghurt

1 cup thick unsweetened yoghurt

1/2 cup sour cream

2 tbsp runny honey

Combine all ingredients. Keep refrigerated until ready to serve. Makes 1 1/2 cups.

Dried Fruit Compote

Dried fruits have a wonderfully intense flavour. Play around with the flavours by adding ingredients to the syrup – try fresh ginger, cardamom pods, star anise or cinnamon quills.

Prep time: 5 minutes + 30 minutes standing

Cook time: 20 minutes

3 cups water

1 cup sugar

400g mixed dried fruits, eg pitted prunes, dried apricots, dried pears, apple slices or fig halves

juice and finely grated rind of 1 lemon

Place water and sugar in a pot and bring to a simmer. Add fruits, lemon juice and rind and simmer over low heat for 20 minutes.

Stand for at least 30 minutes. Serve warm or chilled. Fruit will keep for several weeks in the fridge.

Serves 6-8.

Rockmelon and Raspberries

The efforts of nature and the grower go into creating the perfect fruit. With all the hard work done, your sole contribution is a little ritual in serving.
Here are some favourite combinations:

- Rockmelon halves filled with raspberries
- Rockmelon wedges with glace ginger and lemon juice
- Diced watermelon with blackberries and mint leaves
- Mixed berry bowl drizzled with honey
- Berries with brown sugar
- Fresh figs and raspberries
- Pear wedges with passionfruit pulp and honey
- Sliced oranges and strawberries dusted with sugar
- Grapes, pears, walnuts and honey
- Apples, cheddar cheese and fresh walnuts
- Oranges, grapes, pears and fresh dates
- Persimmons, kiwifruit, passionfruit and ginger
- Fresh pineapple, sliced kiwifruit, passionfruit pulp and sugar
- Fresh pears and figs, ricotta cheese, walnuts and honey
- Pawpaw and lime juice

Lemon and Currant Pancakes

These light-as-air pancakes make a fun start to the day. They are equally good cold or hot, filled with whipped cream and fresh berries for a special treat.
Prep time: *3 minutes*
Cook time: *8-10 minutes*

1 cup self-raising flour

1 cup milk

2 tbsp sugar

$\frac{1}{2}$ tsp baking soda

pinch salt

2 eggs

finely grated rind of $\frac{1}{2}$ lemon

3 tbsp melted butter

1 cup currants or blueberries

Blend all ingredients, except butter and currants, to make a smooth batter. Beat in butter and currants.

Lightly grease a heavy frypan and cook a ladleful of mixture at a time, tilting the pan to spread batter evenly into a large pancake.

Cook over a medium heat. As bubbles form, turn to cook other side. Makes 7-8 large pancakes. Serve hot or cold with whipped cream or yoghurt.

Serves 4.

Eggs Benedict with Smoked Salmon

Weekends are the time for a little luxury, which this dish certainly delivers. Try it with ham, pastrami or bacon.

Prep time: *5 minutes*
Cook time: *5 minutes*

2 bagels, cut in half
4 fresh farm, preferably free-range eggs
4 slices smoked salmon
freshly ground black pepper
1/2 cup hollandaise sauce (see page 108)
GARNISH – watercress

Toast bagels. Keep warm.
Poach eggs.
Arrange smoked salmon on bagels. Top with poached egg. Sprinkle freshly ground black pepper over egg.
SERVE with cheat's hollandaise sauce (see page 108) and garnish with watercress.

Serves 4.

Smoked Salmon Scrambled Eggs

The last word on scrambled eggs – creamy curds with folds of rich smoked salmon.
Prep time: *10 minutes*
Cook time: *6-8 minutes*

4 fresh farm, preferably free-range eggs
2 tbsp water or cream
salt and freshly ground pepper to taste
2 tbsp butter
2 tbsp fresh, soft herbs, eg basil, parsley, tarragon or chervil
6-8 slices smoked salmon, cut thinly

Beat eggs and water or cream lightly with a fork. Season to taste with salt and pepper.
Heat butter in a large, heavy frypan and, when it starts to brown, add the eggs all at once. Sprinkle over fresh herbs.
Cook over medium-high heat, lifting egg as it sets on the base.
Fold in smoked salmon slices. As soon as eggs are creamy throughout (about 1 1/2 minutes), remove from heat and serve on 2 warmed plates.
Do not leave on the stove or the eggs will turn rubbery.

Serves 2.

Spanish Omelette with Potatoes and Bacon

This winning omelette will readily become part of your regular repertoire. Any kind of ingredient can be added to the base mixture of potatoes and eggs – a great way to use up leftovers.

Prep time: 10 minutes

Cook time: 10-12 minutes

2 tbsp olive oil

2 potatoes, diced into 1cm chunks

2 rashers bacon, diced

1 tsp crushed garlic

6 eggs, lightly beaten

3 tbsp chopped parsley

Heat oil in heavy frypan with a heatproof handle.

Add potatoes, bacon and garlic. Cook over a medium heat for 5-7 minutes or until potatoes are just tender. (If using cooked potatoes, add to pan once bacon is cooked and allow to heat through.)

Beat eggs in a large bowl. Mix in herbs.

Pour potato mixture into eggs, season and mix well to combine. Reheat frypan.

Pour mixture into pan and cook over a low heat for 6-8 minutes until three-quarters set. Place under a preheated grill and cook for 5 minutes or until golden brown and set.

Leave for 5 minutes before turning out. Serve warm or cold, cut into wedges.

Serves 4.

Variations

Spinach and Red Pepper – delete bacon and add $1/2$ cup finely chopped, cooked spinach; 1 roasted red pepper, cut into strips.

Seafood – delete bacon and add 200g fresh fish fillets, diced into 2cm chunks (or diced, cooked mussels); 200g surimi; $1/4$ cup parmesan cheese and 1 tsp dried tarragon.

Eggs Benedict

with Smoked

Salmon

Bag yourself a Bagel

Move over pizza, here comes the bagel (in America, bagel joints are opening faster than pizza parlours!). Bagels begin life with a hot water bath, then they're baked, with a turn at half time. This unique cooking process makes them chewy, moist and moreish. Sweet or savoury, they just love a good filling.

- **Pastrami**, *mustard, gruyere cheese and salad greens*

- *Rare roast beef, horseradish sauce, tomato and salad greens*

- *Cream cheese and sun-dried* **tomato pesto**

- *Cream cheese, smoked ham and lightly cooked asparagus*

- **Smoked chicken** *and pesto mayonnaise*

- *Smoked beef, olive paste and brie*

- *Corned beef, mustard and apple*

- *Roasted pepper,* **salami** *and cream cheese*

- *Hummus, red pepper and tomatoes*

- *Shrimps,* **cream cheese** *and pesto*

- *Avocado, ham and sprouts*

- **Mayonnaise**, *olive paste and tomato*

Brunching

with

Bagels

Ultimate French Toast

French toast can taste extra special with a touch of maple syrup. Go on treat yourself, it's so easy.

Prep time: 5 minutes

Cook time: 8-12 minutes

$1/2$ cup milk

$1/2$ cup sugar or liquid honey

3 eggs

1 tsp vanilla essence

finely grated rind of $1/2$ orange

6-8 thick slices french bread or white bread

butter to cook

TO SERVE – bananas, grilled bacon, maple syrup

Beat milk with sugar to dissolve. Beat in eggs, vanilla essence and orange rind.

Dip slices of bread into the liquid to coat both sides.

Heat butter in a heavy pan over a medium heat and cook pieces 2-3 at a time, turning as they brown to cook the other side. Makes 6-8 pieces.

Accompany each serving with several slices of firm banana, cooked bacon and real maple syrup.

Serves 3-4.

Note: French toast can be reheated successfully in oven. Place cooked slices on paper towel and heat in a 200°C oven for 5-8 minutes until the slices start to puff.

Hash Browns

To make crunchy, crisp hash browns, you need a good waxy potato.

Prep time: 5 minutes

Cook time: 16-20 minutes

4 large waxy potatoes, eg fianna, iwa, sabago

salt and freshly ground pepper to taste

a little anchovy sauce to taste

about $1/2$ cup olive oil for cooking

Scrub potatoes, peel if desired and boil for 10 minutes.

Drain and allow to cool. Grate coarsely. Season and, if desired, add a little anchovy sauce.

Heat 2 tbsp olive oil in a heavy pan. Drop handfuls of potato into pan. Flatten with a spatula.

Cook over medium heat until golden, then turn to cook other side (about 8 minutes per side).

Serves 4.

VARIATIONS –
Add sliced cooked corned beef, shredded smoked chicken, or pieces of smoked salmon to the potato mixture before cooking.

Mussel and Zucchini Fritters

Substantial, tender fritters are the result of keeping the batter as thick as possible. Play around with your own favourite combinations. Chef Rodney Dawson, who used to cook at the restaurant downstairs from our office, regularly whips up these fritters and has created a myriad of variations.

Prep time: 10 minutes

Cook time: 16-20 minutes

2 medium eggs

1/2 cup flour

24 cooked mussels, tongues removed

2 tbsp each finely sliced spring onion, chopped coriander and mint

1 tsp finely chopped garlic

1/2 cup grated zucchini

salt and freshly ground pepper to taste

a little lemon juice to taste

a little butter to cook

Mix eggs and flour to make a thick, smooth batter. Cut each mussel into approximately 3 pieces. Add to batter with spring onion, coriander, mint, garlic and zucchini, combining well.

Season with salt, pepper and lemon juice.

Heat butter in frying pan until starting to bubble. Spoon piles of 3 tablespoons of mixture into pan. Flatten slightly to make into fritters.

Cook over a medium heat for approximately 2 minutes on each side.

SERVE fritters with aioli and salad leaves tossed in vinaigrette, sprinkled with a few sea salt crystals.

Makes 12 fritters.

VARIATIONS – in place of mussels and zucchini
Banana Fish Fritters – use 300g diced, fresh boneless fish and 1/2 diced, firm banana
Corn and Pepper Fritters – use 1 cup corn kernels, 1 diced red pepper and a pinch of chilli powder.

Ultimate

French Toast

great

WHO DO YOU KNOW WHO ISN'T BUSY, WHO ACTUALLY HAS TIME TO

sit down to three square meals a day? These days, even your mother is

tied up with seminars, night classes and mountain biking

ADVENTURES. She certainly doesn't have time to turn on the

comfort food every time you're in the mood. Personal trainers may be the

vogue, but few of us can afford our own personal caterer.

    To avoid wasting away, or relying on the local takeaway bar for your

daily sustenance, you need to equip yourself with a whole pile of 'fixings'.

Then, next time you find yourself DINING ON THE

WING, you'll be able to whip together a tasty, nutritious snack in no

time at all. Fill the fridge with yummy nibbles – cheeses, chutneys, sliced meats

and dips – for one-plate put-togethers.

    For almost instant gratification, start with a base of fresh bread,

toasted bread or bread grilled with a brushing of olive oil. Top, fill

or accompany with a combination of your favourite ingredients. In a

couple of minutes you have got bruschetta, cheesy melts, or

FOCACCIA sandwiches – proof that snacking can be glamorous.

Antipasto

Platter

Page 25

grazing

22

great grazing...

Feta and Olive Plate

Next time you fancy a quick snack or mini meal, reach for the feta and olives – and this easy recipe.

Prep time: 10 minutes

1 block feta cheese, cut into chunks
1/2 cup black Ligurian or Calamata olives
1/4 cup extra virgin olive oil
1 tsp crushed garlic
sprig of fresh rosemary, leaves chopped
TO SERVE – wedges of toasted pita bread

Combine all ingredients in a bowl or jar.

SERVE with wedges of toasted pita bread.

Mixture can be left to marinate in the refrigerator for several weeks, provided it is fully covered with oil.

Bring back to room temperature before serving.

Feta and Fennel Spread

Here's another scrumptious spread that exploits the versatility of feta cheese.

Prep time: 10 minutes

Cook time: 3-4 minutes

1 tbsp fennel seeds
250g feta cheese, roughly chopped
3 tbsp olive oil
3 tbsp water
salt and freshly ground pepper to taste

Toast fennel seeds in a dry frypan over medium heat until they start to pop.

Place on a chopping board and roughly crush with rolling pin.

Combine in a blender with all other ingredients, adding a little water to thin.

Store in refrigerator until ready to use. Mix well. Keeps several weeks with a film of oil on top.

Makes about 1^1/$_2$ cups.

Marinated Olives

Marinating olives makes a huge difference to their flavour. Any combination of herbs and spices can be added to an oil base, but these are two of my favourites. If you like, add wedges of cheese to the marinade – colby, cheddar, mozzarella and feta all absorb flavours well.

Prep time: 5 minutes + marinating

Black Olives

Drain black olives from brine and rinse.

Place in jars with 3-4 garlic cloves, peeled and smashed, and fresh rosemary leaves or a couple of dried chillies to taste. Cover with olive oil.

Leave at least 1 week before serving. Olives will keep for months in oil mix. Use oil for cooking or in salads.

Green Olives

Drain green olives from brine and rinse.

Place in jars with finely grated rind of 1 orange and 2-3 lightly crushed cardamoms. Cover with olive oil.

Leave at least 1 week before serving. Olives will keep for months in oil mix. Use oil for cooking or in salads.

Antipasto Platters

- *Chunks of* **feta cheese** *– drizzled with olive oil and fresh rosemary or thyme leaves.*

- *Tinned* **artichoke hearts** *– drained, quartered and mixed through with a tablespoon of vinaigrette dressing.*

- **Button mushrooms** *– mixed with $1/4$ cup garlic vinaigrette dressing. Leave to marinate in fridge for at least four hours.*

- *Wedges of* **Spanish Omelette** *– with bacon and red peppers or spinach and feta cheese.*

- *Thinly sliced smoked meats – smoked* **venison**, *smoked beef, smoked chicken, smoked lamb.*

- *Your* **favourite** *dips and spreads – hummus, black olive spread, white bean spread, Tuscan chickpea spread.*

- **Cucumber batons** *– cut cucumber lengthwise into strips. Toss with freshly ground pepper and lemon juice.*

- *Roasted peppers, sun-dried tomatoes,* **marinated** *olives.*

- *Selection of salad ingredients – snowpea shoots, cherry tomatoes, salad greens, blanched asparagus, baby carrots.*

- *Your favourite cheese,* **pickles** *and chutneys.*

Bruschetta

Cut thickish slabs of a dense country loaf, brush with olive oil and bake until semi-crisp and pale golden. Cover with desired toppings and serve or quickly grill to heat through. Try the following topping combinations:

- **Smoked** fish, olive oil, crumbled feta cheese and shredded spring onions.
- **Olive** paste or tapenade, sliced canned artichokes, grilled with havarti or other semi-soft cheese.
- **Crumbled** grilled bacon, finely diced mushrooms, seasoned mayonnaise to bind and a little lemon juice, then grilled.
- **Pastrami**, spicy tomato relish, roasted sliced peppers and zucchini, bound with a little prepared tomato pasta sauce and topped with mozzarella.
- **Sun-dried tomato** paste, sliced tomatoes and olives.

Blue Boursin Cheese Spread

Some people find blue cheese a bit strong. Adding cream cheese and fresh herbs transforms it into a smooth, mild spread that suits all palates.
Prep time: 5 minutes

250g cream cheese
100g blue cheese
1 tsp crushed garlic
2 tbsp chopped, fresh, soft herbs, eg oregano, basil, tarragon, parsley
juice of 1/2 lemon
salt and freshly ground pepper to taste

Blend all ingredients until smooth.
SERVE at room temperature. Mixture will keep in refrigerator for several days.
Makes about 2 cups.

Bruschetta

topped with

Blue Boursin Cheese

Spread, Tuscan

Chickpea Spread &

Feta and Fennel

Spread

White Bean Crostini with Broccoli Greens

I try to keep a stock of several cans of white beans on hand to whip up this creamy, nutritious spread. Here I have served it on toasted french bread with cooked broccoli greens for a light meal, but it makes a great stand-alone spread.

Prep time: 15 minutes

Cook time: 4-5 minutes

310g can white beans, rinsed and drained

3 tbsp good quality olive oil

1 clove garlic, crushed

1 bay-leaf

sprig of fresh thyme, or pinch dry thyme

juice of 1/2 lemon

salt and freshly ground pepper to taste

TO SERVE – 1 head broccoli, toasted french bread, coarse/country bread or focaccia

Place beans in a microwave bowl or saucepan with olive oil, garlic, bay-leaf and thyme.

Microwave covered on 50% power for 4 minutes, or cook in a saucepan over low heat for 5 minutes.

Lift out and discard bay-leaf and thyme (if using fresh) and puree mixture in a blender with lemon juice, salt and pepper.

Peel broccoli, divide into segments and cook in a little water with 1 teaspoon olive oil until tender. Drain, cool, then dice finely and season with black pepper.

Pile bean puree onto a platter with broccoli to the side. Accompany with a pile of toasted bruschetta or french bread. To serve, spread bean puree on each side of toasted bread and top with broccoli.

Serves 2.

Tuscan Chickpea Spread

A quick whizz in the blender and the humble chickpea is transformed into a yummy dip.

Prep time: 10 minutes

310g can chickpeas, drained and rinsed

2 large, ripe tomatoes, roughly chopped

2 cloves garlic, crushed

2 tbsp herb pesto

2 tbsp olive oil

2 tbsp white wine or tarragon vinegar

salt and freshly ground pepper to taste

Puree all ingredients in a blender to a semi-smooth consistency.

Canned beans can be used in place of chickpeas. Mixture will keep in the refrigerator for 24 hours.

Makes about 1 cup.

Salsa

This traditional Mexican salsa combines sweet, juicy tomatoes with chillies, garlic and fresh coriander. Serve it with barbecues, corn chips, fresh bread or meatballs.

Prep time: 2 minutes

5 large, ripe tomatoes, or 400g can tomatoes in juice, roughly chopped
1/2 small onion, very finely diced
1 tsp crushed garlic
1/2 red pepper, diced
1 tsp chilli paste or hot chilli sauce to taste
2 tbsp finely chopped coriander or mint
salt and freshly ground pepper to taste
pinch of sugar

Place all ingredients in a food processor and blend until semi-smooth.

SERVE at room temperature. Salsa will keep for several days in refrigerator.

Makes 1½ cups.

Traditional Guacamole

The trick to making good guacamole is to find good quality avocados. Don't use them when they have become soft and brown. The flesh should be semi-firm and green. The avocado is ready to use if it gives when cradled in your hands, or if the stem presses in easily where it attaches to the skin.

Prep time: 5 minutes

2 large ripe avocados, mashed with a fork
1 tsp crushed garlic
2-3 tbsp lemon juice to taste
3 tbsp chopped coriander
salt and freshly ground pepper to taste
pinch of chilli powder or 2-3 drops tabasco
1 tomato, diced finely
2 tbsp finely chopped onion or spring onion
small handful coriander or parsley, stems removed and finely chopped

Mix all ingredients until well combined.

SERVE with corn chips, vegetables bites or as an accompaniment to grills. Mixture browns easily, so make just before using. Keeping the stone in helps prevent browning.

Makes about 1 ½ cups.

Salsa and

Traditional

Guacamole

Cobb Sandwich

Layering bacon, cooked chicken, salad vegetables and blue cheese between fresh buns or focaccia makes a meal of this great sandwich.

Prep time: 10 minutes

Cook time: 5 minutes

1 large fresh bun or piece of focaccia bread

2 tbsp mayonnaise mixed with 1 tsp
   mustard

1 rasher bacon, cooked until crispy

2-3 very thin slices cooked chicken or
   sliced turkey

$1/2$ tomato, thinly sliced

$1/2$ avocado, peeled and sliced

3-4 crisp lettuce leaves, washed and dried

1 tbsp crumbled blue cheese

Split bun or focaccia and toast cut surfaces.

Spread one side with mayonnaise, assemble other ingredients on top in layers as listed.

Top with other half of bun, spread with flavoured mayonnaise.

Serves 1.

Flavoured Mayonnaise

For best results, use a homemade mayonnaise as a base. Flavoured mayonnaises are good for dipping, filling or spreading. They will keep for several days in the refrigerator.

Prep time: 10 minutes

Pesto Spread

Mix 2-3 tbsp pesto with 1 cup mayonnaise.

Tapenade Spread

Mix 3-4 tbsp tapenade or olive paste with 1 cup mayonnaise.

Sun-dried Tomato Spread

Mix 1 tsp crushed garlic and 3 tbsp minced sun-dried tomatoes in oil with 1 cup mayonnaise.

Make a sandwich with ...

- Smoked ham, swiss cheese and sun-dried tomatoes.
- Chicken, ham and pan-fried mushrooms.
- Brie, ham and mushrooms.
- Roast beef and dill mustard.
- Pastrami, cream cheese and sun-dried tomatoes.
- Salami, dill, cucumber and swiss cheese.
- Spinach and feta cheese.

Aioli

Essentially a very garlicky mayonnaise, aioli is the ultimate accompaniment for grilled or boiled vegetables and chicken or seafood-based salads. It will keep in the refrigerator for up to a month.

Prep time: 10 minutes

6 large cloves garlic, peeled
4 egg yolks
juice of 1 large lemon
salt and freshly ground pepper to taste
1/2 tsp each sugar and mustard powder
about 2 cups virgin olive oil

Place all ingredients, except oil, in a food processor. Puree until smooth.

With motor running, add oil in a slow stream until mixture thickens to a heavy spooning consistency.

Check seasoning and adjust if required. Store in refrigerator.

Makes about 2 cups.

VARIATIONS –

Puree a large handful of herbs, eg parsley, rocket or basil, in with garlic.

Le Grand Aioli

SERVE with cooked white beans and pepper, cucumber, boiled baby potatoes, cooked green beans, raw or slightly sauteed florence fennel, roasted peppers and grilled eggplant.

Black Olive Paste

This delicious mix will keep forever in the refrigerator – but it never lasts that long. Add a couple of spoonfuls to salad dressings, spread onto bread or bruschetta with sliced tomatoes, or toss through cooked pasta with tomatoes, spinach and parmesan.

Prep time: 5 minutes

1 cup tasty black olives
1/4 cup capers, rinsed
2 tbsp olive oil
juice of 1/2 lemon

Press olives to loosen stones. Remove stones and puree in a food processor or pound in a mortar with all other ingredients. Mix will keep indefinitely in the fridge. Recipe doubles easily.

Makes 3/4 cup.

Marinated

Green Olives

Focaccia Melts

Tender, flavoursome focaccia bread makes a great base for updates on the cheese-on-toast theme. Split the bread through the middle, top with your favourite topping combinations and finish with cheese. Quickly grill until the cheese melts. If preferred, the cheese can be grilled atop the bread for a more dramatic presentation.

Smoked Chicken and Avocado Melt

Brush the cut surfaces of bread with garlic-flavoured oil or garlic butter and lightly grill.

Top with slices of smoked chicken, sliced avocado, a drizzle of lemon juice, grated mozzarella and freshly ground black pepper.

Grill until cheese melts.

Cajun Chicken Melt

Season a chicken breast with cajun spices and pan fry.

Split focaccia bread and brush with garlic flavoured oil or garlic butter. Top with sliced tomato, sliced avocado and cooked chicken. Sprinkle with cheese.

Grill until cheese melts. Top with remaining bread.

Eggplant,

Pesto and

Avocado Melt

Pesto, Bacon, Avocado and Tomato Melt

Spread cut surface of bread with pesto.

Top with cooked bacon, slices of avocado and grated mozzarella.

Grill until cheese melts.

Eggplant, Pesto and Avocado Melt

Preheat grill.

Slice 1 eggplant into 1cm rounds.

Brush slices with oil and grill for 2-3 minutes each side until golden and soft.

Split focaccia. Spread one half with pesto, then arrange layers of cooked eggplant, sliced avocado and sprouts. Sprinkle with cheese.

Grill until cheese melts. Top with sprouts and remaining bread.

New Season

Asparagus and

Parmesan

cheese

page 42

sexy salads...

Greek Chicken Salad with Tapenade Dressing

Toss cooked, shredded chicken flesh with tapenade dressing to lightly coat. Add wedges of tomatoes, red and green peppers, cucumbers, sliced spring onions, feta cheese and salad greens.

Prep time: 15 minutes

1/2 cooked chicken (flaked flesh) – remove skin, bones and fat, slice flesh

2 tomatoes, cut in wedges

1 red and/or green pepper, cut into chunks

4cm piece cucumber, cut in batons

100g feta cheese, diced

2 large handfuls salad greens

DRESSING

1/2 cup olive oil vinaigrette dressing

1 tsp crushed garlic

1 egg yolk

2 tbsp tapenade or black olive paste (see page 31)

Prepare all salad ingredients.

Shake salad dressing ingredients to combine.

Toss quarter of dressing through salad greens and divide between 2 plates.

Mix rest of dressing with remaining ingredients and pile onto greens.

Serves 2.

Chicken, Pear and Watercress Salad

A quick toss in the pan with some chicken, then onto a bed of watercress with pears and walnuts. Great for a lunch or a picnic.

Prep time: 10 minutes

Cook time: 4-5 minutes

400g chicken tenderloins

2 tbsp olive oil

juice of 1/2 lemon

salt and freshly ground pepper to taste

6 large handfuls watercress, washed and dried

2 tbsp vinaigrette dressing

2 pears, peeled, cored, sliced in wedges

1/2 cup fresh walnut pieces

Mix chicken with oil, lemon juice and salt and pepper.

Heat frypan and cook chicken over a medium-high heat, tossing frequently, for 4-5 minutes until cooked.

Mix watercress with vinaigrette to coat and divide between 4 plates. Pile chicken fillets on top and garnish with pears and walnuts.

Serves 4.

Pesto, Corn and Chicken Salad

This salad sings of summer. Make it when corn and basil are at their peak.

Prep time: 15 minutes

1 cup whole kernel corn

1 large avocado, peeled and diced

3 tomatoes, quartered

2 spring onions, finely sliced

400g fresh green beans

1 size 6 cooked chicken (or 1 smoked chicken), remove skin and fat, dice flesh

DRESSING

1/2 cup vinaigrette dressing

2 tbsp pesto

Drop beans into a pot of boiling water for 1 minute, drain and cool under cold water.

Place with other salad ingredients in a bowl.

Combine dressing ingredients and mix well. Toss through the salad. Serve with fresh bread or bruschetta.

Serves 4.

Smoked Chicken and Peach Salad

Smoked chicken is a very useful standby, great for sandwiches, salads and melts. Here I have combined it with fresh peaches, but any seasonal fruit could be used.

Prep time: 15 minutes

DRESSING

6 tbsp olive oil

1/4 cup white wine vinegar

2 tsp grainy mustard

1 tbsp honey

juice of 1 orange

salt and freshly ground pepper to taste

SALAD

flesh of 1 smoked chicken, shredded

2 peaches, halved, stones removed and sliced

1/4 honeydew melon, cut into batons

2 stalks celery, sliced

GARNISH – salad greens, sprigs of fresh mint

To make the dressing, combine all ingredients and mix well. Combine salad ingredients in a mixing bowl. Gently toss through dressing.

SERVE – divide salad between 5 individual plates. Garnish with a few salad greens and a sprig of fresh mint.

Serves 5.

Grilled Chicken Salad with Citrus Chilli Sauce

Inspired by Anita Lo, the divine dressing for this salad is best prepared at least 12 hours in advance. It's wonderful on all types of seafood, as well as chicken and meat.

Prep time: 15 minutes

Cook time: 2-3 minutes

DRESSING

juice of 1 orange

juice of 2 limes or lemons

3 tbsp rice wine vinegar

2 tbsp Vietnamese fish sauce

$1/2$ tsp hot chilli sauce

1 clove garlic, crushed

1 tbsp sugar

salt and freshly ground pepper to taste

3 boneless, chicken breasts, sliced thinly

salt and freshly ground pepper to taste

2 tbsp each minced coriander and mint

8 handfuls of fresh, mixed salad greens

GARNISH – $1/2$ red onion, finely cut; 3 oranges, segmented; 1 large avocado, cut into wedges

Combine all dressing ingredients and refrigerate for at least 12 hours (up to 1 week in the fridge).

Mix oil through chicken and season with salt and pepper. Briefly cook on a preheated grill or hot frypan – do not overcook.

Toss dressing with any cooking juices. Wash and dry salad greens.

Drain a little of dressing into washed salad greens and toss to coat.

Gently toss through red onion, orange segments and avocado. Divide greens between 6 plates and top with chicken. Spoon over remaining dressing.

Serves 6.

Grilled Chicken

Salad with

Citrus Chilli Sauce

Grilled Scallops and Asparagus Salad

Scallops and asparagus are the first of spring's many treats. Celebrate the new season with this special salad.

Prep time: 15 minutes
Cook time: 2 minutes

1 large kumara, cut into thick matchsticks

400g fresh scallops

salt and freshly ground pepper

3 tbsp olive oil

finely grated rind of 1/2 orange (no pith)

3 oranges, peeled and segmented

1 large avocado, cut in wedges

12 - 16 spears asparagus, boiled 2 minutes

6 large handfuls salad greens, washed

juice of 1 orange and 1 lemon

GARNISH – fresh coriander leaves and
   pepper

Prepare all ingredients, cook asparagus, wash salad greens, etc.

Heat a small pot with 4-6cm oil and fry kumara sticks until golden. Drain thoroughly and place on paper towels.

Season scallops with salt and pepper and mix through orange rind and olive oil.

Heat a barbecue grill or frypan and cook scallops over high heat for 1 minute each side. Remove from heat and toss in combined orange and lemon juice.

Toss salad greens with scallops and orange segments and citrus juices.

Divide between 4 serving plates and garnish with asparagus and avocado.

GARNISH with coriander and grinds of black pepper.

Serves 4.

Grilled Scallops

and Asparagus

Salad

With a Summer's Tomato

Find the sweetest, juiciest summer tomatoes, then:

- *Slice, drizzle with extra virgin olive oil, a little balsamic vinegar, sprinkle with sugar and black pepper.*

- *Layer with slices of fresh mozzarella and basil leaves, drizzle with virgin olive oil.*

- *Rub a piece of good-quality rustic bread with garlic. Halve a ripe tomato and rub into bread to coat. Drizzle with olive oil. Sprinkle over rock salt.*

- *Split a fresh loaf of bread and scoop out a little of the soft bread on one half. Fill with layers of sliced tomatoes, olives and feta. Replace the top and weight down for an hour before slicing and serving.*

- *Puree with a little pesto, season and toss with cooked spaghetti.*

- *Toss with batons of cucumber, sliced red onions, diced peppers, chopped mint and vinaigrette dressing.*

- *Dice and mix with black olives, sliced red pepper and garlic. Quickly toss in a pan with olive oil and freshly ground pepper to heat through. Mix through cooked pasta with a couple of spoonfuls of black olive paste.*

Fresh Tomatoes with

Balsamic and Olive Oil

Smoked Salmon Pasta Salad with Capers, Eggs and Herbs

A little goes a long way. Rich, densely flavoured salmon makes a perfect partner for pasta in this easy salad.

Prep time: 15 minutes

Cook time: 10 minutes

500g dried Italian pasta

200g smoked salmon pieces

1/4 cup salad oil, eg safflower or soya

2 tbsp lemon juice

finely grated rind of 1/2 lemon (no pith)

1 tbsp capers

a good handful of fresh mixed herbs, eg
parsley, chervil, basil, mint

1 bunch spinach, washed and shredded

salt and freshly ground pepper to taste

GARNISH – 4 hard-boiled eggs, 2 finely
sliced spring onions, sprinkling of capers

Cook pasta according to manufacturer's instructions.

Prepare dressing by blending a third of salmon with oil, lemon juice, rind, capers and fresh herbs.

Drain cooked pasta. Toss through dressing and leave to cool.

Before serving, toss in rest of smoked salmon and shredded spinach. Season to taste. Pile onto a salad platter and garnish.

Serves 6.

Take 5 – Great matches for salad put togethers

Wash and dry a selection of salad greens, allowing a big handful per serve.

Drizzle over 2 parts olive oil to 1 part balsamic vinegar. Season with salt, pepper and a pinch of sugar.

Take One – toss with orange segments, crisp bacon and sliced avocado.

Take Two – toss with grapes, spring onion, toasted cashews and brie.

Take Three – toss with flaked, warm grilled salmon, avocado and capers.

Take Four – toss with bacon, bananas, avocado and croutons.

Take Five – toss with sliced, grilled chicken, red peppers, olives and pesto.

New Season Asparagus

Snap the crispest asparagus, discarding ends. Boil for 2 minutes, drain and cool under cold water. Allow about 6-8 spears per serve. Then ...

- drizzle over virgin olive oil, grind over black pepper and, using a vegetable peeler, shave over parmesan cheese.

- serve with a big bowl of garlicky aioli.

- toss with segments of oranges and toasted cashews and dress with orange juice blended with roasted cashew nuts.

Caesar Salad

Give this timeless salad your own signature by adding grilled chicken or shrimp, olives or cherry tomatoes. Once made the dressing will keep for a couple of days in the refrigerator.

Prep time: 10 minutes

leaves of two romaine or other crisp
  lettuces
12 - 18 french bread croutons
black pepper
DRESSING
6-8 anchovies
1 tsp crushed garlic
1/2 cup olive oil
2 egg yolks
3 tbsp lemon juice
1/4 cup cream
grated parmesan cheese

Wash and dry lettuce leaves.

Mash together anchovies and garlic, then mix together with remaining ingredients.

Toss dressing through salad greens and garnish with croutons. Grind over black pepper.

Serves 6.

Chicken Caesar –
Grill 2 chicken breasts and slice into salad while still warm.

Shrimp Caesar –
Rinse 400g fresh shrimps and pan-fry in garlic oil. Toss through salad while still warm.

Caesar Salad

with French Bread

Croutons

Wilted Greens, Coriander and Peanuts with Sesame Dressing

An exotic way to get your share of greens for the day.
Prep time: *10 minutes*
Cook time: *3-4 minutes*

1 cup oil, eg peanut or soya
1 cup peanuts
2 large bunches fresh coriander leaves,
stripped from stems
1 medium iceberg lettuce, shredded
DRESSING
2 tbsp soy sauce, preferably Japanese
2 tsp sesame oil
1 tsp sugar
1/2 tsp salt

Heat oil in small pot until it is nearly smoking.
Add peanuts, stir and turn off heat. Stand for about 3-4 minutes until golden, then drain and place on paper towels to remove excess oil.
Pour boiling water over coriander leaves, drain immediately, squeeze out the excess moisture and chop finely (the coriander will shrink to about a handful).
Mix with peanuts and lettuce. Combine dressing ingredients and toss through salad.

Serves 4-6.

Cantonese Salad Parcels

A refreshing Asian taste experience.
Prep time: *10 minutes*
Cook time: *10 minutes (approximately)*

80g vermicelli or egg noodles
oil to deep fry
1 tbsp sesame or hot sesame oil
400g lean pork, diced very finely or minced
150g green beans, sliced thinly
OPTIONAL – 1/4 cup or 1 can water
chestnuts, rinsed and sliced
1 tsp finely chopped fresh root ginger
1/4 cup oyster sauce
about 2 small crisp iceberg lettuces,
trimmed, washed, excess water shaken
out and cut in half

Divide noodles into 4 parcels. Deep fry in batches until crisp, but not brown. (Alternatively, you can use already-prepared crispy fried noodles.)
Drain on paper towels.
Heat sesame oil in large pan or wok and stir-fry pork, beans, water chestnuts and ginger over a high heat for 2-3 minutes until beans are just cooked.
Mix in oyster sauce. Combine stir-fry and noodles and divide between 4 dinner plates, placing half a head of lettuce on each plate. Each person wraps their own parcels.

Serves 4.

Spicy Bean and Vegetable Roll-ups

Flat bread, such as mountain bread and Persian naan bread, makes a useful wrapper for salad-style fillings.
Prep time: 15 minutes

310g can chilli beans
2 tsp cumin
1/2 cup sour cream
2 tbsp fresh chopped coriander or parsley
salt and freshly ground pepper to taste
OPTIONAL – extra chilli sauce

Puree all ingredients together. Add a little extra chilli sauce if you prefer a hotter mixture.
Roll up mountain breads, fill with a couple of tablespoons of the mixture, top with alfalfa sprouts, batons of cucumber, peppers and sliced avocado.

Makes 4 large rolls.

Persian Pinwheels

Spread a sheet of flat bread with bands of different filling ingredients, then roll and slice 4-5cm pieces for any-time snacking.

- Hummus, tabbouleh, red pepper and smoked beef.
- Cream cheese, smoked salmon, cucumber and snowpea sprouts.
- Cream cheese, dried apricots and spinach.
- Smoked fish, red pepper, sour cream and gherkin.
- Ham, mashed egg, spinach and green olives.
- Pineapple, berries, ginger, honey and sour cream.
- Blue cheese, walnuts, and grapes.

Persian

Pinwheels

barbecues

For a nation of ardent barbiephiles, we're lousy outdoor cooks. *Speed overrules prudence and, in the race to get it all on the table, the rules of good grilling are forgotten; avoid raw flame, control the* H E A T *source and avoid contaminants such as kerosene, turps and treated charcoal. Burnt meat contains a host of gene- damaging chemicals that may or may not be rendered harmless in the human digestive tract. Avoid these potential carcinogens by following these easy rules for food that is juicy,* S U C C U L E N T *, lightly smoked and golden crusted.*

Undoubtedly, the best flavours in grilling are achieved by using wood embers. Chips of manuka, fruit woods or grapevine cuttings, lightly soaked in water for 30 minutes, or fresh bundles of herbs, such as R O S E M A R Y *, can impart delicious flavours to delicate, mild foods, such as chicken, fish and vegetables. Sprinkle the soaked wood-chips or herbs over the heat source just before commencing cooking. If any flare-ups occur, wait for them to die down before you add the food.*

Hotter than

Hell Barbecue

Prawns

Page 52

grills

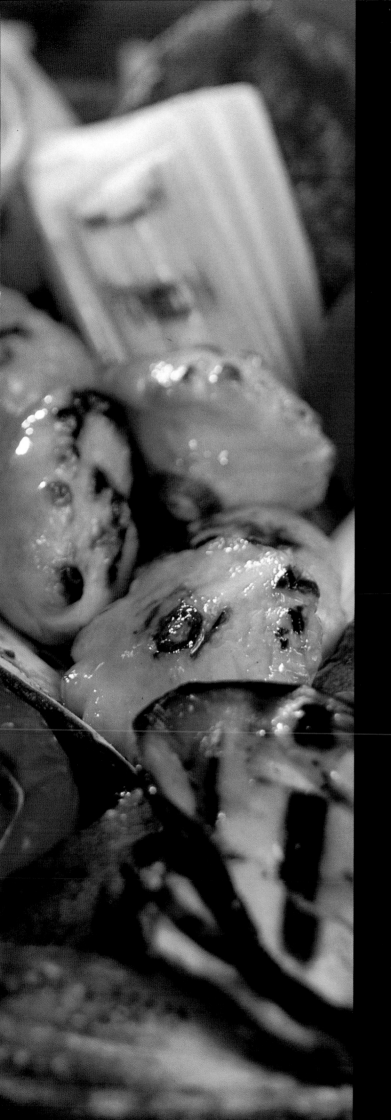

barbecues & grills...

Grill-Smoked Vegetables

A big platter of richly flavoured vegetables lashed with garlicky aioli makes a wonderful meal for any kind of outdoor dinner or barbecue picnic. Take care not to char foods, because the blackened areas are unpalatable and unhealthy.
Prep time: 15 minutes
Cook time: 5-15 minutes

1-1.5kg of a variety of seasonal vegetables, eg peppers, mushrooms, eggplant, corn, zucchini, tomatoes, fennel, potatoes, leeks
about $1/4$ cup olive oil
2 cloves garlic, crushed
rock salt and freshly ground pepper to taste

Prepare vegetables.
Preheat a barbecue grill rack.
Mix oil and garlic. Brush generously over all vegetables and season lightly with rock salt and black pepper.
Cook over medium heat until tender and lightly golden, turning and brushing with oil 2-3 times during cooking.
Drizzle or sprinkle grilled vegetables with aioli or olive oil, chopped herbs and balsamic vinegar or lemon juice, toasted pinenuts and parmesan cheese.

Serves 6-8.

Barbecue Preparation for Grilled Vegetables

CORN – if very fresh, leave in husks. *Soak* in cold water 10-20 minutes. *Grill* 20-30 minutes. If corn is older, husk and cut into 4-6cm chunks. *Boil* 3 minutes, then barbecue until heated through and lightly golden.

EGGPLANT and PEPPERS – *Slice* into thin rounds and cook 8-10 minutes.

MUSHROOMS – Choose flat mushrooms with brown gills. *Wipe* clean, brush with oil and place, gill-side up, on hotplate or barbecue. Cook 5-8 minutes.

LEEKS, ONIONS and ZUCCHINIS – Use baby leeks left whole. *Cut* large leeks and zucchinis lengthwise and *cut* onions into rounds or wedges. Cook 15 minutes.

POTATOES, KUMARA and FENNEL – cut in 1.5cm-thick slices. *Boil* for 5 minutes, then drain thoroughly before oiling and barbecuing. Cook 10-15 minutes.

Grilled Chicken and Red Pepper Sandwich with Olive Mayonnaise

Hot, juicy chicken, fresh bread, olive mayonnaise and crisp salad vegetables come together to make one of my favourite meals-on-the-run.
Prep time: 5 minutes
Cook time: 8-10 minutes

2 chicken breasts or 4 chicken thighs

2 tbsp olive oil

salt and freshly ground pepper to taste

1 red pepper, seeds removed and cut in thick slices

2 pieces focaccia bread or baps

olive mayonnaise

salad ingredients, eg tomato, cucumber, spinach leaves, avocado, etc

Lightly pound chicken breasts between plastic wrap to flatten.

Preheat olive oil on a barbecue grill or frypan. Season chicken and fry over medium-high heat with red pepper until cooked through.

While chicken is cooking, split 2 pieces of focaccia bread, lightly toast and spread with olive mayonnaise on each side.

Sandwich hot chicken into bread with slices of fresh tomato and cucumber, spinach leaves, avocado, sprouts, etc.

Serves 2.

Felafels

Buy felafel mix or make your own using canned chickpeas and this easy recipe.
Prep time: 5 minutes
Cook time: 10 minutes

310g can chickpeas, rinsed and drained

1 tsp crushed garlic

2 tsp ground cumin

pinch cayenne

juice of 1/2 lemon

2 tbsp tahini

salt and freshly ground pepper to taste

a little oil to cook

1 tbsp parsley

Puree all ingredients together in a food processor or finely mash chickpeas and combine with other ingredients. Use wet hands to form into balls the size of a large walnut. Flatten into small patties.

Heat a little oil on a barbecue hotplate or frypan and fry patties on both sides over medium heat until golden. Makes 8-10.

Serves 2.

Mussels with a Fresh Herb Crust

Fresh breadcrumbs and herbs combine with olive oil to form a crispy crust that also serves to keep the mussels moist and tender. Serve hot or cold, alone or as part of a buffet.

Prep time: 5 minutes
Cook time: 5-6 minutes

4 thick bread slices, crumbed (1½ cups)
2 tsp crushed garlic
¼ cup fresh chopped herbs, eg parsley, basil
2 tbsp olive oil to moisten
24-30 mussels in half shell, cooked, or live mussels frozen until opened

If using live mussels, freeze for an hour or two until opened (they can be frozen up to a week in advance).
Remove top shell and beard and place in a single layer in a baking dish.
Blend breadcrumbs with garlic, herbs and oil.
Sprinkle generously over mussels on the half shell.
Place under a preheated grill until mussels are cooked and breadcrumbs are crisp and golden – 5 minutes if using precooked mussels, or bake at 250°C for about 10 minutes if using raw mussels.

Serves 4-6.

Hotter Than Hell Barbecue Prawns

Choose large, whole, green prawns for this sensational taste treat. Take care not to overcook and serve with garlic aioli, crusty bread and a mixed green salad for a fast fresh meal.

Prep time: 5 minutes + 10 minutes marinating
Cook time: 3-4 minutes

12 - 16 raw big prawns, eg Tiger Prawns
1 ½ - 2 tsp Cajun spice mix
2 tbsp olive oil
2 cloves garlic, crushed
2 tbsp chopped fresh coriander
1 lime, halved
salt and freshly ground pepper to taste

Mix prawns with all ingredients and marinate for 10 minutes before cooking.
Heat barbecue grill or frypan.
Cook prawns over medium-high heat for about 3-4 minutes until prawns are pink and cooked through. Test one by breaking it off at the head – if the flesh is no longer translucent, the prawn is cooked through.
While prawns cook, place lime halves, cut-side down, onto grill plate for 2-3 minutes to soften.
SERVE immediately, with bread or rice and a salad.
Accompany with finger bowls of warm water and lemon slices. Recipe easily doubles or triples.

Serves 2.

Chargrilled Whole Fish

Any fresh whole fish cooks wonderfully on the barbecue. Take care not to overcook – the eye of the fish should just be white and the flesh only just starting to flake when pierced in the deepest part.

Prep time: 15 minutes

Cook time: 20-25 minutes

1.2-1.5kg whole fresh fish
(cleaned, gutted and scaled)
1 bunch fresh herbs
1 lemon, sliced thinly
1 tbsp olive oil
salt and freshly ground pepper to taste

S l a s h fish deeply on the diagonal 3-4 times on each side, season cavity and place herbs and lemon inside.

L i g h t l y oil and preheat barbecue. Rub oil into fish.

C o o k over a medium heat, about 10cm above heat source, for 5 minutes. Carefully turn and cook a further 15-20 minutes, loosely covered with tinfoil.

S e r v e s   2 .

Rock Oysters with Spinach and Bacon

Oysters freeze very well, so buy extra for the freezer when you happen on a really fresh supply.

Prep time: 10 minutes

Cook time: 4-5 minutes

12 fresh or frozen oysters on the half shell
1 tbsp olive oil
2 rashers bacon, finely chopped
2-3 heads fresh spinach, washed and dried
2 tbsp cream or sour cream
salt and freshly ground pepper to taste

H e a t oil in a pan. Fry bacon until it starts to brown.

S l i c e spinach, add to pan and cook until wilted.

M i x in cream or sour cream and stir until evenly incorporated. Season to taste.

S p o o n mixture onto oysters. Place under preheated grill for 4-5 minutes until oysters are just set.

S e r v e s   2 .

Rock Oysters

with Spinach

and Bacon

Unbeatable Burgers

Burgers can be anything you want them to be, and you don't have to head for the local takeaway every time you need a fix. By using spicy chicken, bacon and avocado, chilli beef, or crisp fish and tartare sauce, gourmet home-made burgers can be put together in a flash. Keep a supply of buns in the freezer and be ready to satisfy your next burger urge.

Prep time: 5 minutes
Cook time: 4-6 minutes

300g lean steak mince

salt and freshly ground pepper to taste

4 rashers bacon

TO ASSEMBLE

4 hamburger buns

your choice of sliced tomato,

lettuce or spinach leaves

avocado wedges, sprouts, cucumber,

beetroot, peppers, mayonnaise,

chilli sauce or relish

Season meat with salt and freshly ground black pepper. Use wet hands to shape into 4 balls. Flatten into patties 1.5-2cm thick.

Preheat a barbecue hotplate, oven grill or frypan. Barbecue, grill or fry for 2-3 minutes each side. Fry bacon until crisp.

Split buns and toast. Spread cut surfaces of each half with mayonnaise. Arrange layers of ingredients on top of bun. Top with other half of bun.

Serves 4.

Gourmet Burger Combos

Cajun Burger – add 2 tsp ground cumin and 1-2 tsp chilli powder to raw beef and assemble with chilli sauce and gherkins.

Chicken Burger – use 300g chicken mince or 4 boneless chicken thighs, season with salt and freshly ground black pepper, 1 tsp ground cumin and $1/2$-1 tsp chilli (or to taste).

Satay Burger – make a chicken burger and top with avocado, spring onions and peanut sauce.

Chicken and Camembert Burger – make a chicken burger and top with camembert, cooked bacon, avocado, orange slices and watercress.

Salad and Fish Burger with Lemon Mayonnaise – season boneless fish fillets with salt, freshly ground pepper and a little Cajun spice. Fry in a little butter to cook. Fill into burger with salad greens and mayonnaise flavoured with chopped gherkins and lemon juice.

Finger-licking Ribs for Two

Share these sticky, moreish ribs with a friend – and be prepared to get messy!

Prep time: 5 minutes + marinating

Cook time: 40 minutes

750g short, meaty, pork or beef ribs

1/4 cup sugar

2 tbsp honey

2 tbsp dry sherry

2 tbsp hoisin sauce

Combine sugar, honey, sherry and hoisin sauce in a large bowl.

Mix in ribs. Cover and refrigerate for 3-6 hours, turning occasionally.

Bake covered at 180°C for 30 minutes, then uncover and bake a further 10 minutes. Recipe doubles easily.

Serves 2.

Chicken Fajitas

Pronounced "far heetas", these tasty Mexican treats can be prepared successfully using any type of thinly sliced meat, poultry or seafood. Make up your own Cajun spice mix or buy one of the commercial ones.

Prep time: 5 minutes + 5-10 minutes marinade

Cook time: 10 minutes

400g boneless chicken breasts or thighs,
  cut in thin strips

1 tbsp oil

1 tsp crushed garlic

2-3 tsp Cajun spice mix

1 red pepper, sliced in thin strips

1 red onion, sliced in thin wedges

salt and freshly ground pepper to taste

8 pita bread halves

Mix chicken with all other ingredients and stand for 5-10 minutes before cooking.

Preheat a barbecue hotplate or frypan.

Cook large handfuls of chicken and vegetables for 10 minutes over a medium-high heat – about 5 minutes on each side, frequently turning until chicken is cooked through. Do not overcrowd hotplate. Turn frequently.

Remove from heat. Fill into toasted pita bread halves, mountain bread or warmed tortillas.

Garnish with a dollop of guacamole and lettuce leaves.

Makes 8 pockets.

Lemon and Herb Chicken Drumsticks

The Mediterranean flavours of garlic, fresh rosemary, lemon and olive oil are a favourite match for chicken. Great hot or cold, these drumsticks make perfect picnic fare.

Prep time: 5 minutes + marinating

Cook time: 15-20 minutes

8 chicken drumsticks

¼ cup olive oil

3 tbsp lemon juice

1 tsp crushed garlic

1 tbsp fresh chopped rosemary leaves

salt and freshly ground pepper to taste

1 lemon halved, cut into very fine slices

OPTIONAL – ½ cup green olives and several fresh sage leaves

Combine chicken with all other ingredients, except lemon slices, olives and sage leaves. Marinate for at least 15 minutes.

Preheat barbecue grill plate. Lift chicken from marinade. Cook for about 8-10 minutes per side. Alternatively, microwave drums in covered container for 6-7 minutes, then barbecue grill for 5 minutes each side.

Sprinkle over lemon slices (and optional olives and sage leaves) in the last 5 minutes of cooking to prevent overcooking.

Serves 4-6.

Pesto Chicken Breasts with Eggplant and Red Pepper

Vegetables and chicken combine deliciously in this mixed grill. Other seasonal vegetables can be used as available, such as zucchinis, leeks and kumara. Play around with various types of pesto – mint or coriander, for example.

Prep time: 10 minutes

Cook time: 8-10 minutes

2 skinless, boneless chicken breasts or 4 boneless thighs

juice of ½ lemon

3 tbsp olive oil

2 tbsp prepared pesto

salt and freshly ground pepper to taste

1 eggplant, sliced into 1cm rounds

1 red pepper, cut into thick wedges

Place chicken breasts between 2 sheets of plastic wrap. Lightly pound to flatten to 1.5cm.

Combine lemon juice, oil, pesto, salt and pepper and brush over chicken, eggplant and pepper slices.

Preheat a barbecue grill plate or large frypan and lightly oil. Cook chicken, eggplant and pepper until chicken is cooked through.

SERVE with aioli, oven fries and a crisp green salad.

Serves 2.

Spicing up your Barbecue

There was a time – before the advent of food processors and microwaves, single-parent families and gobble-and-go lifestyles – when life was simple, ingredients were basic, cooking took forever and eating was dull.

Enter sun-dried tomatoes, fish sauce, balsamic vinegar, wasabi and other exotic flavour-packed ingredients. These intense tastes have launched cooking into a new realm. Here's the low-down on some of our favourite new flavour experiences:

SUN DRIED TOMATOES – intensely flavoured, sold either dried or packed in olive oil. **Uses** – slice into pastas, boost casseroles and soups, add to salads, puree to make pestos, serve as part of mixed platters.

FISH SAUCE – the essence of South-East Asian cooking. Wonderfully cheap, it keeps forever. Known variously as nam pla (**Thailand**), nuoc mam (**Vietnam**), tuk trey (**Kampuchea**), patis (**Philippines**) and ngan pya ye (**Burma**). Fish sauce smells dreadful, but it's a brilliant flavour booster. **Uses** – Try it instead of soy sauce in Asian-style stir-fries, add $^{1}/4$-$^{1}/2$ cup to your favourite Thai curry, mix into marinades for chicken or pork, use as base for a fat-free dressing for green and other salads – using equal parts fish sauce and lime or lemon juice.

CAJUN SPICE MIX – this versatile spice combination adds life to grills and barbecues. Use commercial mixes, like Paul Prudhommes, or make your own using 5 parts each paprika and ground cumin, 3 parts garlic powder, 2 parts each chilli powder, salt and brown sugar, and 2 parts either dried rosemary or fennel seeds. Use about 3 tbsp per 500g to season or marinate meat, fish or poultry.

BALSAMIC VINEGAR – aged for a minimum of 20 years before it hits the shelf, balsamic vinegar comes in numerous grades – older is usually better and more expensive. **Uses** – infinitely versatile. Toss through a green salad with extra virgin olive oil and black pepper for a stunning dressing, add a dash to finish a soup, drizzle over fresh sliced tomatoes, use in salad dressings or mayonnaise instead of regular vinegar.

Chicken

Fajitas

out*Of* t h e

Food from the oven has its own special virtues. It reminds us of the days when someone stayed at home to look after us. It has a smell that says "welcome", make yourself at home.

Oven cooking is what I call carefree cooking. The dish goes into the OVEN and, when it is cooked, you take it out. There's no need to hover around stirring and fussing. Unless your oven is of the ancient, temperamental VARIETY, your food will emerge perfectly cooked, without a lot of worrying on your part. The oven's dry heat allows food to caramelise, creating great colour and added flavour.

Most oven-cooked food has good lasting power. Unlike "eat-me-now" stir-fries and pasta dishes, oven-cooked dishes generally taste just as good hours later. They freeze well, too.

Next time you want to say "I care", turn on the oven and whip up a batch of TENDER muffins or a tasty savoury pie.

French
Potato Pie
page 72

oven

Gourmet pizza

Combinations

Page 71

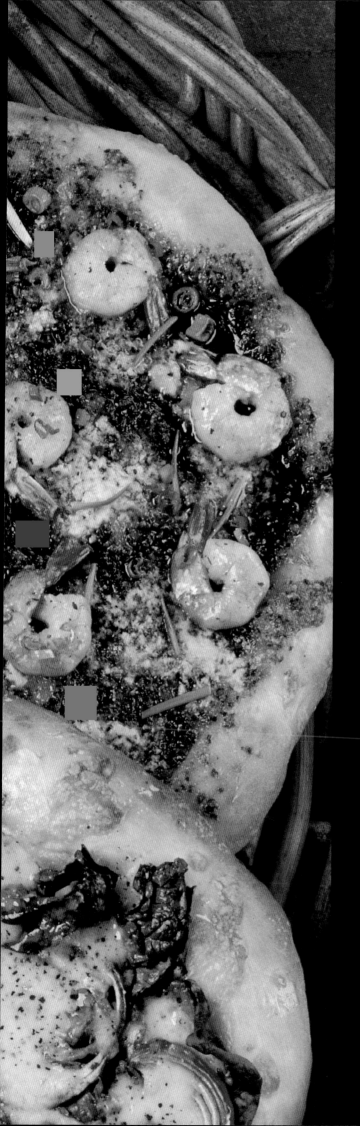

Blueberry Muffins

Better than anything at the local bakery, these light fruit muffins are a weekend favourite.

Prep time: 5 minutes

Cook time: 15-20 minutes

100g butter, melted

1 cup brown sugar

2 eggs

1/2 tsp baking soda

1/2 cup milk, warmed

1 tsp vanilla essence

1 ripe banana, mashed

2 cups self-raising flour

2 cups blueberries, fresh or frozen

TOPPING – 1/4 cup sugar mixed with 1 tbsp cinnamon

Preheat oven to 200°C.

Beat together butter, brown sugar and eggs.

Dissolve baking soda in milk. Mix milk, vanilla essence and banana into butter mixture.

Fold in flour and blueberries, mixing until just combined. Do not overmix.

Divide mixture between 12 greased muffin tins.

Sprinkle with sugar mixture. Bake at 200°C for 15-20 minutes. Stand for 5-10 minutes before removing from tins.

Makes 12 muffins.

Yoghurt, Cheese and Bacon Muffins

This easy recipe forms the base for a myriad of flavour inventions.

Prep time: 5 minutes

Cook time: 20-25 minutes

2 cups self-raising flour

2 tsp baking powder

1/2 tsp salt

1/4 tsp chilli powder

2 cups grated tasty cheese

2 rashers bacon, diced, cooked

1 egg

1 cup plain yoghurt

1 cup milk

Preheat oven to 200°C.

Combine all dry ingredients with the cheese and bacon.

Beat egg, yoghurt and milk together just to combine and mix quickly and lightly into the dry ingredients. (The mixture should be quite wet.)

Spoon mixture into 12 greased muffin tins. Bake at 200°C for 20-25 minutes until puffed and golden. Stand for 5-10 minutes before removing from tins.

Makes 12 muffins.

Avocado and Bacon – add 2 rashers diced, cooked bacon plus 1/2 avocado, diced.

Fruity Bran Muffins

These light, tender muffins deliver a painless fix of fibre in a flash.

Prep time: 10 minutes

Cook time: 20 minutes

1 1/2 cups plain flour

1 1/2 tsp baking powder

2 cups bran flakes

2 tsp ground cinnamon

2 cups chopped fruit, eg berries, bananas

50g butter

3/4 cup brown sugar

3 tbsp golden syrup

1 1/2 cups milk

1 1/2 tsp baking soda

Preheat oven to 180°C.

Combine flour, baking powder, bran flakes and cinnamon in a large mixing bowl with fruit.

Heat butter, sugar, golden syrup and milk in microwave until dissolved. Stir in baking soda.

Stir liquid ingredients into dry ingredients, mixing lightly. Do not overmix. Divide mixture between 12 greased muffin tins.

Bake at 180°C for 20 minutes.

Makes 12 large muffins.

Scones with a Twist

Use your favourite scone recipe with some new taste sensations – make pinwheel scones or twists with ingredients like pesto, tapenade or sun-dried tomatoes.

- Prepared pesto and finely grated mozzarella cheese.
- Tapenade, anchovies and finely grated mozzarella.
- Bacon, rosemary, grated gruyere and freshly ground pepper.
- Fennel seeds and gruyere cheese.
- Feta cheese, olives and tapenade.
- Sun-dried tomatoes, garlic, cheese and chilli.
- Freshly grated apple, cinnamon, dates and finely grated orange rind.
- Bananas, chutney and cheese.
- Bananas, glace ginger and brown sugar.
- Dried apricots, figs and walnuts.
- Ground almonds, fennel seeds, hazelnuts and honey.
- Brown sugar, cinnamon and chocolate chips.

Life's a Hot Potato

Often called 'poor man's truffles', potatoes are one of the world's greatest foods – nutritious, tasty and oh, so satisfying.

Jacket Potatoes

Prep time: 10 minutes
Cook time: 1 hour

4 large potatoes, scrubbed with skin on
1/4 cup sour cream
salt and freshly ground pepper to taste
filling of your choice (see below)

Bake potatoes at 200°C for 1 hour until soft.
Use a sharp knife to cut a cross in the top of each potato, squeeze in sides to open out.
Spoon over sour cream and filling of your choice.
SERVE at once.

VARIATION –

Cut a slice from the top and scoop out the flesh, leaving the jacket intact.
Place flesh in a bowl. Mash with 1 tbsp sour cream per potato and flavouring ingredients of your choice. Refill cut potato shells and return to oven or microwave to heat through.

Potato Fillings and Flavourings

- Crispy cooked, diced bacon and spring onions.

- Red pepper, salami and sun-dried tomatoes.

- Feta cheese, tapenade and rosemary.

- Pesto and cheese.

- Curried chicken, watercress and avocado.

- Colbasse sausages and asparagus.

- Blue vein and walnuts.

- Smoked salmon and brie cheese.

- Smoked salmon, capers and red onions.

- Ham and crushed pineapple.

- Smoked fish and chives.

Baked Jacket

Moroccan Potato Wedges

The secret life of the potato is exciting and exotic, spiced with the flavours of north Africa.

Prep time: 10 minutes

Cook time: 20-25 minutes

4 medium/large baking potatoes, eg ilam hardy, nadine, russet

2 tbsp oil

1 tbsp tomato paste

1 tbsp cumin seeds, toasted

2 tsp paprika

pinch cayenne

1/2 tsp black pepper

1 tsp garlic salt

Scrub potatoes and cut into wedges about 1.5cm thick. Place in a baking dish and mix through oil and tomato paste.

Toast cumin seeds in a dry pan until they pop. Tip onto a board and grind with a rolling pin. Mix with other spices.

Sprinkle over potatoes, turning to coat evenly.

Bake at 220°C for 20-25 minutes until golden and crunchy.

Serves 2-4.

Mediterranean Wedges – Prepare wedges as above. In place of spice mix, cook with 2 tbsp chopped, fresh rosemary leaves and 1 tsp rock salt. In the last 15 minutes of cooking, add 2 finely sliced cloves garlic and 1/2 cup tasty black olives.

Seedy Wedges – Prepare wedges as above. Mix through oil, then sprinkle with either sesame, poppy or fennel seeds.

Leek Tart

Leeks, cream, eggs and cheese are a great combination for lunch or picnic eating. Other vegetables and ingredients – like bacon, chicken or blue cheese – can be added to the egg and cream base.

Prep time: 40 minutes

Cook time: 20 minutes

1 x 23-25cm cooked savoury pastry crust
  (see page 108)
2-3 sliced leeks
butter to cook
$1/2$ cup cream
2 eggs
$1/4$ cup parmesan cheese
$1/2$ cup grated gruyere or blue vein cheese
salt and freshly ground pepper to taste
pinch of nutmeg

Cook leeks in plenty of butter over low heat until soft.

Mix cream with eggs. Add leeks, parmesan and grated gruyere or blue vein cheese.

Season with salt and pepper and a little nutmeg.

Pour into prepared pastry crust and bake at 200°C for 20 minutes until filling is set and lightly golden.

Serves 6-8.

Mexican Sausage Slice

This spicy savoury pie slices well and is ideal for transporting.

Prep time: 20 minutes

Cook time: 40 minutes

2 sheets puff pastry
200g lean beef, minced
200g sausage meat
50g hottest salami, diced into 5mm cubes
2 tsp chilli powder
1 tsp ground cumin
2 tsp garlic, crushed
$1/2$ cup finely chopped parsley
OPTIONAL – 1 cup sliced green olives
salt and freshly ground pepper to taste
GLAZE – 1 egg beaten with 1 tbsp water

Press 1 sheet of pastry into a small, greased roasting or deep baking dish (20cm x 20cm) to cover base, and 2cm up the sides.

Mix all filling ingredients in a bowl and spread over pastry base. Use wet hands to smooth top.

Brush with egg wash and bake at 200°C for 10 minutes. Reduce heat to 180°C for a further 30 minutes until puffed and golden.

SERVE in wedges, either hot or warm.

Serves 4-5.

Vegetable Stuffed Naan Breads

Commercial naan mix makes fast work of these samosa-styled breads.

Prep time: 15 minutes

Cook time: 10 minutes

1 pkt naan bread mix

2 tbsp prepared pasta tomato sauce

2 cups cooked vegetables, such as potato, pumpkin, kumara, peas, celery

1 tsp each curry powder, ground cumin, ground coriander, garlic salt, fennel seed a pinch of cinnamon, cloves and chilli powder

salt and freshly ground pepper to taste

Preheat oven to 180°C.

Make naan bread mix and prepare to manufacturer's instructions.

Mix cooked vegetables with spices and seasonings. Combine with tomato sauce to bind.

Divide bread dough into four pieces and roll out thinly. Fill one side with mixture, then fold over, seal and bake for 10 minutes, turning once during cooking.

Serves 4.

Cheesy Oven-baked Gnocchi with Corn and Spinach

Serve it hot, serve it cold – either way this cheesy bake is a winner.

Prep time: 5 minutes

Cook time: 23-35 minutes

1 litre milk

50g butter

1 1/4 cups semolina

3 eggs, lightly beaten

2 cups grated tasty cheese

1/4 cup parmesan cheese

1/2 tsp fresh grated nutmeg

1 cup whole kernel corn, drained and rinsed

1 1/2 - 2 cups cooked spinach, excess liquid squeezed out and diced

salt and freshly ground pepper to taste

Heat milk and butter until it just comes to boil.

Add semolina and stir until the mixture boils and turns very thick.

Remove from heat and quickly beat in eggs, cheese, nutmeg, corn, spinach and seasonings.

Spoon mixture into a well-greased, shallow casserole dish (about 26cm).

Bake at 200°C for 25-35 minutes until top is golden and crispy. To serve, spoon out of dish, or allow to cool and serve in slices.

Serves 4-6.

Traditional Neapolitan Pizza Crust

This recipe is adapted from "The Italian Baker". It has a light, airy texture, and is good for both deep-dish pizza and flat pizzas. The more you stretch the dough when shaping it, the finer it becomes and the more crunch you get on cooking. Raw dough freezes well.

Prep time: 20 minutes + rising

Cook time: 15-25 minutes

1 ³/₄ tsp active dry yeast or 12g fresh yeast

pinch sugar

1 ¹/₃ cups warm water

¹/₄ cup olive oil, plus additional for brushing
   the crust

3 ³/₄ – 4 cups all-purpose flour

1 ¹/₂ tsp salt

Stir yeast and sugar into water in large mixing bowl. Stand 5 minutes until foamy. Stir in oil.

Mix flour and salt and add 1 cup of yeast mixture at a time, beating well to get all lumps out.

Knead on a lightly floured surface until soft and satiny but firm – about 8 minutes.

Roll ball of dough around in an oiled bowl to coat it with oil. Tightly seal bowl with plastic wrap and set aside in a warm, draft-free place. Let dough rise until not quite double in size, 30 to 45 minutes.

Divide dough into balls if making more than 1 pizza. Flatten ball until 5mm thickness for crispy pizza, or 2cm thickness for deep-dish pizza. Place dough in an oiled pizza tray. Cover with desired toppings and bake.

Gourmet Pizza Combinations

Use **pizza** dough or pita breads as a base. Bake at 250°C for crispy pizzas and 220°C for thicker deep-dish pizzas. Bake until cheese is melted and bases are **crisp** or golden brown – about 15-25 minutes for dough bases, 8-10 minutes for pita bases.

- **Red** Pepper, Artichoke and Salami – Sprinkle base with mozzarella. Top with artichoke halves, thinly sliced red pepper, sliced red onion and salami. Sprinkle over **mozzarella** and black pepper.

- Pesto and **Blue Cheese** – Spread base with pesto. Crumble over blue cheese, finely sliced red onion and top with shrimps. Grate over a little mozzarella.

- **Goats' Cheese**, Mushrooms and Olive – Spread base

Bacon and Egg Pie

Great for a picnic, served either warm or cold.

Prep time: 5 minutes

Cook time: 35-40 minutes

2 sheets ready rolled flaky puff pastry

2 rashers bacon, finely diced

8 eggs

salt and freshly ground pepper to taste

2 tomatoes, sliced

Line a shallow baking tin with pastry, slightly overlapping the edges where the pastry joins. Trim to fit tin, reserving extra pastry for lattice top.

Sprinkle diced bacon and any optional additions over pastry, then break the eggs directly onto pastry shell. Lightly prick yolks with a fork and spread out evenly to cover pastry. Top with slices of tomato.

Cut remaining pastry into thin strips about 1cm wide, and arrange in a criss-cross pattern on the top of pie.

Bake in a preheated 220°C oven for 10 minutes, reduce heat to 180°C and cook a further 25-30 minutes until golden, puffed and set.

Serves 5-6.

OPTIONAL ADDITIONS –

Pesto, onion, broccoli, cooked rice, cooked diced potato, and drained, flaked tuna.

French Potato Pie

This satisfying pie is guaranteed to convert the most ardent meat eater.

Prep time: 15 minutes

Cook time: 55 minutes

500g savoury shortcrust pastry

1kg potatoes, peeled and thinly sliced

1 large spanish onion, peeled and sliced

2 tbsp oil

4 eggs

300ml cream

2 tbsp dijon mustard

salt and freshly ground pepper to taste

60g tasty cheese, grated

3 tbsp finely chopped parsley

Preheat oven to 190°C. Lightly grease bottom of a 25cm ovenproof pie dish. Roll pastry out thinly. Cover base and sides of dish, reserving enough for top.

Boil or microwave potatoes for 5 minutes. Drain and pat dry. Fry onions gently in oil until softened.

Fill pie dish with alternative layers of potato and onion, finishing with a layer of potatoes.

Beat eggs, cream and mustard. Season with salt and pepper. Pour over potato and onion layers. Sprinkle over cheese. Cover with pastry and seal.

Brush with milk or beaten egg to glaze.

Bake in oven for 55 minutes or until golden brown and potatoes are tender.

Serves 6.

Greek Spinach Roll

This herby brew of spinach and feta cheese and encased in a crisp pastry crust, is great for holidays, weekends and picnics.

Prep time: 15 minutes

Cook time: 35 minutes

2 tbsp olive oil

1 small onion, finely chopped

400g spinach, washed, stems removed and trimmed, cooked, excess liquid squeezed out, chopped

1 egg, lightly beaten

200g cottage cheese

100g feta cheese, crumbled

$1/4$ cup grated parmesan cheese

2 tbsp chopped parsley

$1/2$ tsp nutmeg

salt and freshly ground pepper to taste

3 sheets or 400g flaky pastry, thinly rolled

Heat oil and cook onion over low heat until soft.

Add to all other ingredients, except pastry.

Roll out pastry to a 35cm x 25cm rectangle. (If using pre-rolled pastry, overlap it, brushing with a little egg-wash to join.)

Lay spinach mixture in a band along bottom edge. Roll up to fully enclose filling, allowing about 3cm overlap. Seal edge with egg wash and place roll, joined edge down, on baking sheet. Use any remaining pastry to garnish. Brush with a little milk or beaten egg.

Bake at 200°C for approximately 35 minutes, or until pastry is golden brown.

Serves 4-6.

Greek

Spinach Roll

*O**n**e*

FOR MANY OF US, TRYING TO RUN ABOUT THREE LIVES AT

once, the week-night evening meal can turn into a gobble of

straight sustenance. Add the requirement to deliver good

NUTRITION, *with the prescribed 5+ vegetables and a*

ration of lean protein, and the evening plate can become awesomely

dull. It can seem that your only choice is whether to mash the

potatoes or leave them whole.

Stove-top one-pot meals, such as stir-fries, pasta and soup,

are one of the least time-consuming ways to cook dinner.

Ingredients are added during the cooking process, depending on the

time they need. These types of meals lend themselves to ethnic

influences and lots of creative licence. If you haven't got any black

bean sauce, try oyster sauce. If the recipe says to SEASON

with coriander, but you'd prefer mint, then go for it. At the end

there is only one pot to clean.

Be prepared to pay a premium for quality ingredients. When

time is not on your side, you need the best raw materials you can

find to CREATE *memorable meals. Seek organic ingredients*

wherever you can find them – treat yourself to their pure, chemical-

free flavours.

Fresh

Tomato Pasta

page 78

ot hot

Fettuccine with

Scallops and

Pesto

Page 79

76

Fettuccine with Rustic Tomato and Chicken Sauce

Spike a jar of commercial pasta sauce and simmer some sliced chicken for a whizz-together, one pot dinner.

Prep time: 5 minutes

Cook time: 18-20 minutes

400g fettuccine

1 tbsp oil

1 tsp each crushed garlic and hot chilli sauce

2 cups prepared tomato pasta sauce

1 cup white wine

salt and freshly ground pepper to taste

pinch sugar

400g boneless chicken, cut in thin strips

2 tbsp prepared pesto

Cook pasta according to manufacturer's instructions.

Heat oil in a large pan and cook garlic and chilli sauce for 1 minute. Add pasta sauce, wine and seasonings and bring to a simmer.

Simmer over a low heat for 10 minutes. Add chicken, cover and simmer for 8-10 minutes until chicken is cooked.

Mix through the pesto. Toss sauce through cooked, drained pasta.

Serves 4.

Fresh Tomato Pasta with Peppers and Olives

When tomatoes are sweet and juicy, make this easy pasta toss.

Prep time: 10 minutes

Cook time: 12-15 minutes

400g penne pasta or pasta shells

6 large fresh tomatoes, roughly chopped

2 tsp each tomato paste and crushed garlic

1 tsp sugar

a good shake tabasco or pinch of chilli powder

1/4 cup virgin olive oil

1 red pepper, finely diced

12-16 black olives

salt and plenty of freshly ground pepper

Cook pasta according to manufacturer's instructions. While pasta is cooking, prepare sauce.

Place all ingredients – except olive oil, red pepper and olives – in a blender bowl, and blend well.

Heat oil and fry red pepper and olives for 1-2 minutes until pepper softens. Add tomato sauce to pan and stir just to heat through. Season to taste.

Drain pasta and toss through sauce.

Serves 4.

Fettuccine with Scallops and Pesto

The luxurious taste of scallops holds its own in this quickly prepared pasta dish.

Prep time: 10 minutes

Cook time: 8-10 minutes

400g fettuccine
400g-600g scallops
salt and freshly ground pepper to taste
2 tbsp butter
1 clove garlic, crushed
juice of 1 juicy lemon
3/4 cup basil, watercress or parsley pesto
GARNISH – spring onion curls, finely grated
   rind of 1/2 lemon

Cook pasta according to manufacturer's instructions.

If short on scallops, slice in half. Season with salt and pepper.

Heat butter in heavy frypan. When it bubbles, add scallops and garlic.

Toss over high heat for about 1 1/2 minutes until scallops are just cooked.

Drain cooked pasta and toss with lemon juice and pesto. Toss through scallops and pan juices. Adjust seasoning to taste and garnish with spring onion curls and scrolls of lemon rind.

Serves 4.

Fettuccine with

Rustic Tomato

and Chicken Sauce

Easy Pasta Combos

Spinach, Ricotta and Walnuts – Cook spinach and walnuts in olive oil with a little garlic. Toss through pasta with ricotta cheese and parmesan.

Puttanesca – Fry anchovies, garlic, capers and olives in olive oil, season with chilli and pepper. Toss through pasta with fresh diced tomatoes.

Pepper and Zucchini with Basil Aioli – Fry diced peppers and zucchini in olive oil. Toss through pasta with basil aioli.

Goats' Cheese and Watercress – Cook watercress in olive oil with garlic and chilli. Heat goats' cheese with cream to thin. Toss through pasta and pile greens on top.

Fettuccine Carbonara with Broccoli

Traditional carbonara gets a healthy twist with the addition of broccoli. Spinach is also delicious.

Prep time: 10 minutes
Cook time: 10 minutes

200-300g fettuccine
1 head broccoli, peeled and cut into florets
2-3 rashers bacon, diced
1/2 tsp crushed garlic
1/2 cup cream
2 eggs, lightly beaten
salt and freshly ground pepper to taste
1 spring onion, finely chopped
1/2 cup coarsely grated parmesan cheese

Cook pasta according to manufacturer's instructions.

Add broccoli florets in last 2-3 minutes of cooking.

Cook bacon in a large pan until starting to brown. Add garlic and cream and bring to a simmer.

Drain cooked pasta and broccoli and add to cream, tossing with tongs to combine.

Mix in eggs, salt, black pepper and spring onion.

Pile onto 2 warmed pasta bowls and sprinkle over parmesan.

Serves 2.

Pasta with Blue Cheese and Spinach

Blue cheese melts wonderfully. Here it's combined with cream and spinach for a quick, yummy pasta meal.

Prep time: 5 minutes
Cook time: 10 minutes

400g pasta shapes, eg fusilli
1 cup cream
100g-120g blue cheese, crumbled
1 tbsp olive oil
1 tsp crushed garlic
1 large bunch (6-8 heads) fresh spinach, washed, stems removed and chopped
plenty of freshly ground pepper to taste

Cook pasta according to manufacturer's instructions.

Combine cream and blue cheese in pot or microwave bowl. Heat until cheese has melted.

Heat olive oil with garlic in a heavy frypan. Add spinach and cook until wilted.

Drain pasta and toss through blue cheese cream. Season to taste. Divide between heated bowls and top with spinach.

Serves 4.

VARIATIONS
Goats' Cheese and Spinach – Substitute goats' cheese for blue cheese.
Jalapeno and Spinach – Substitute jalapeno cheese for blue cheese.

Pasta Siciliana

Kumara, orange, nuts and herbs combine in a light tomato and orange sauce.

Prep time: 15 minutes

Cook time: 20 minutes

1 tsp olive oil

1 tsp each crushed garlic and fresh chopped thyme

1kg kumara, peeled and cut into 1cm cubes

pinch of nutmeg

1 cup orange juice

400g can tomatoes in juice, pureed

400g penne pasta or other shaped pasta

$^{1}/_{2}$ cup each toasted pumpkin seeds and grated cheese

$^{1}/_{2}$ cup chopped parsley

salt and freshly ground pepper to taste

GARNISH – $^{1}/_{2}$ cup parmesan cheese, 2 tbsp capers

Heat olive oil in a frypan. Cook seasonings for a few seconds.

Add kumara, nutmeg, orange juice and tomatoes and simmer uncovered over low heat for 20 minutes, or until kumara is tender.

Cook pasta according to manufacturer's instructions, then drain.

Toss through kumara sauce, pumpkin seeds, cheese and parsley. Season to taste. Garnish.

Serves 4.

Pasta

Siciliana

Stir-fried Beef with Straw Mushrooms, Chilli and Mint

As with most stir-fries, the only effort required is at the preparation stage. Leave the cooking until everyone is sitting down to eat.

Prep time: 15 minutes
Cook time: 3 minutes

400g lean beef steaks, sliced thinly across
 the grain into small batons
2 tbsp fish sauce
1 tbsp sesame oil
1 yellow or red pepper, sliced thinly
200g sliced bok choy or Chinese cabbage
1 - 2 fresh chillies, chopped
1 can straw mushrooms or plain
 mushrooms, rinsed and drained
OPTIONAL – snowpeas, bean sprouts
salt and freshly ground pepper to taste
1/4 cup red wine
3 tbsp fresh mint, finely chopped

Prepare meat and all vegetables ready to cook. Mix meat with fish sauce and sesame oil.
Heat a heavy pan and fry meat over a high heat for 2 minutes until just browned.
Add all other ingredients – except seasonings, wine and mint – tossing over heat until cabbage is wilted. Season and mix in wine and mint. Serve at once.
Serves 4.

Stir-fried Chicken with Orange, Ginger and Asparagus

When asparagus is out of season use beans or zucchinis, so you can enjoy this wonderful stir-fry all year through.

Prep time: 10 minutes
Cook time: 6 minutes

500g boneless chicken thighs or breasts,
 skin removed and thinly sliced
2 tbsp oil
2 tsp each crushed garlic and minced root
 ginger
finely grated rind of 1 orange
500g fresh asparagus or beans, angle cut in
 4-5cm lengths
1 red pepper, cut into matchsticks
1/2 cup light soy sauce
1 orange, peeled and cut into segments

Mix chicken with 1 tbsp oil, garlic, ginger and orange rind.
Drop asparagus or beans into a pot of boiling water and cook for 2 minutes. Drain and cool under cold water.
Heat remaining tablespoon of oil in a wok or pan and fry chicken over high heat until browned.
Add asparagus and pepper and toss over heat for 2 minutes. Mix in soy sauce and orange segments.
SERVE on bed of rice or noodles.

Serves 4.

One Quick Curry

Green curry paste, coconut cream and fish sauce form the base for a range of Thai-styled curries.

Prep time: 5 minutes

Cook time: 8-10 minutes

1 tbsp oil

1-2 tbsp green curry paste to taste

400ml can coconut cream

1-2 tbsp fish sauce

500g boneless fish, sliced or

  4 fresh crabs cut in quarters or

  500g boneless chicken thighs, sliced

freshly ground pepper to taste

GARNISH – 4 tbsp chopped coriander

little lemon rind

Heat oil in a pot and fry curry paste for a few seconds.

Add coconut cream and fish sauce and bring to a simmer.

Add seafood or chicken and cook over a low heat (2-3 minutes for fish, 5-6 minutes for chicken and crabs). Season to taste.

GARNISH – with chopped coriander and shavings of lemon rind.

Serves 4.

Vegetable and Tofu Curry –

Scrub 2 potatoes and cut in 3cm pieces. Peel and cut a wedge of pumpkin into 3cm pieces. Cut 200g block of tofu into chunks.

Fry with oil and curry for a few minutes.

Add coconut cream and simmer 5 minutes, then add 1 cup peas or beans and simmer until cooked. Season and garnish.

Chickpea Curry –

Drain and rinse 310g cans chickpeas and white beans.

Fry with oil and curry paste, then add coconut cream and simmer 10-15 minutes.

Season and garnish.

One Quick

Curry

Chilli Tomato and Pumpkin Soup

This is a great recipe for times when there seems to be nothing in the cupboard. If pumpkin is unavailable, you could substitute potatoes or kumara.

Prep time: 10 minutes

Cook time: 10-15 minutes

1 tbsp oil

1 tsp each crushed garlic and chilli powder

2 tsp ground cumin

finely grated rind of 1 orange

400g can peeled tomatoes in juice, pureed

3 cups chicken stock

1 1/2 cups peeled, diced pumpkin

1/4 cup fresh coriander, chopped

salt and freshly ground pepper to taste

Heat oil in a large pot and sizzle garlic, chilli and cumin for a few seconds.

Add all other ingredients, except fresh coriander and seasonings, and simmer for 10-15 minutes until pumpkin is tender.

Season to taste and mix through coriander. Serve at once.

Serves 4.

Chilli Tomato

and Pumpkin

Soup

With a Can in the House

- **Mix** a large can of drained tuna with white sauce, season with lots of lemon juice and chopped parsley. **Top** with mashed kumara and grated cheese and bake to heat through.

- **Heat** a can of tomato soup with an equal amount of water and a dash of chilli sauce. **Make** meatballs with lean mince, crushed garlic, the finely grated rind of 1 lemon, pinch cayenne and salt and pepper. **Roll** into small balls and drop into soup. Simmer until cooked, serve over noodles.

- **Drain** a can of whole kernel corn, fry with a little onion, garlic and the leaves of a sprig of thyme. **Add** a can of tomatoes in juice and some diced pumpkin or kumara. **Simmer** until tender, sprinkle with cheese.

- **Season** a can of chilli beans with 2 tsp ground cumin, 1 tsp chilli and 2 tbsp chopped fresh coriander. **Heat** and serve over a bed of corn chips, sprinkle with grated cheese and melt. **Garnish** with a dollop of sour cream and mashed avocado.

Spicy Seafood Broth

Next time you purchase fresh mussels, try this tasty soup.

Prep time: 10 minutes

Cook time: 7 minutes

1 ¹/2 cups chicken stock

¹/2 cup white wine

finely grated rind of 1 lime or lemon
  (no pith)

400g can tomatoes, pureed

¹/2 - 1 tsp Thai red or green curry paste (or
  more to taste)

1 carrot, peeled and cut into matchsticks

20-24 mussels, in the shell, scrubbed

OPTIONAL – 150g shrimps

2 spring onions, finely sliced

Combine all ingredients – except carrot, seafood and spring onions – in a large pot.

Simmer for 5 minutes.

Add carrot and mussels and cook until mussels open. Discard any that do not open.

Add shrimps, allow to heat through, mix in spring onions and serve.

Serves 4.

Creamy Mussel and Corn Chowder

A chunky, hearty brew – great for a cold winter's night.

Prep time: 15 minutes

Cook time: 15 minutes

2 tsp oil

1 small onion, finely diced

2 rashers bacon, rind removed, finely diced

¹/2 cup white wine

1kg live mussels, scrubbed, beards removed

1 stick celery, diced

2 potatoes, cut into 1cm cubes

1 litre water

310g can creamed corn

300ml milk

2 tsp cornflour mixed with 1 tbsp sherry

salt and freshly ground pepper to taste

¹/4 cup finely chopped parsley

Heat oil in a medium pot and fry onion and bacon over low heat for 8 minutes or until onion is soft.

Add wine and mussels, cover and steam, removing them as they open, then dice, removing beards. Add celery, potatoes and water to pot. Simmer 10-12 minutes until potatoes are just cooked.

Add mussels to pot with corn, milk, combined cornflour and sherry.

Season and bring just to boil. Sprinkle over chopped parsley and serve immediately.

Serves 4-6.

Vietnamese Pho Bo

This substantial staple combines vegetables, noodles and slivers of chicken in a spicy clear broth.

Prep time: 15 minutes

Cook time: 10 minutes

3 cups chicken stock

2 tbsp fish sauce

1 leek, washed and cut in thin rounds

1 chicken breast, skinned and sliced as
   thinly as possible

1 chilli, thinly sliced (or 1 tsp chilli paste)

1 handful clear vermicelli noodles

1 bunch watercress or spinach, stalks
   removed, chopped

2 tbsp chopped fresh mint and/or coriander

salt and freshly ground pepper to taste

juice of 1 lemon or lime

Bring chicken stock to a simmer in a large pot.

Add fish sauce and leeks and simmer for 5 minutes.

Mix in all other ingredients, except watercress and herbs, and simmer 3 minutes until chicken is cooked through.

Mix through watercress and herbs. Season to taste and serve at once.

Serves 2.

OPTIONAL ADDITIONS – Sliced mushrooms, carrots, peppers, tomatoes.

Vietnamese

Pho Bo and

Spicy Seafood Broth

_a_ littl e

There is more than a little P R U D E N C E _about life in_
the `90s. Time, money and the eternal battle of the bulge steer us
clear of any grand finales.   _But you scream, rich cakes,_
T E N D E R _fruity tarts, and moreish slices are part of my_
heritage, they're in my psyche.

At the corner cafe we find ourselves sneakily indulging in
gooey C H O C O L A T E _cakes, which would never dream of_
making ourselves. _But, you don't need an honours degree to create_
great desserts. _A lot of dessert making errs on the side of chemistry_
rather than alchemy. Without a doubt, a master baker is a gifted
technician, but a great many D E L I C I O U S _sweet   treats_
can be prepared with ease, given a good set of scales, a food
processor and a reliable oven. Send everyone to seventh heaven with
this collection of melt-in-the mouth treats.

indulgence

Plum Cake

served

with fresh

whipped cream

page 94

a little indulgence...

Marinated Strawberries in Pinot Noir with Mascarpone

Marinating strawberries really brings out their flavour, and pinot noir – with its natural berry undertones – makes a perfect partner.

Prep time: 10 minutes + 1 hour marinating

Cook time: 2-3 minutes

1/2 cup water

1 tbsp chopped mint leaves

1/2 cup sugar

1 cup pinot noir wine

juice of 1 lemon

3 punnets strawberries, hulled and halved

250g mascarpone

GARNISH – sprigs of mint, shattered brandy snaps

Combine water, mint and sugar in a microwave-proof jug, or pot.

Cook for 2-3 minutes until sugar is fully dissolved. Stir in wine and lemon juice. Cool.

Place strawberries in a bowl, and pour over cooled syrup. Cover and refrigerate for up to 8 hours before serving.

Spoon marinated strawberries into individual serving dishes. Top with a dollop of mascarpone, a sprig of mint and a few pieces of broken brandy snap.

Serves 6.

Cheat's Tart Tatin

Cooked half on the stovetop and half in the oven, this caramelised apple pie is a cinch for even the most novice cooks.

Prep time: 10 minutes

Cook time: 50 minutes

50g butter

1/2 cup brown sugar

6 apples, peeled, cored and cut into thin wedges

finely grated rind of 1 orange or lemon

1/2 tsp ground cloves or cardamom

2 sheets pre-rolled flaky pastry, joined

Preheat oven to 220°C.

Melt butter and sugar in a shallow, ovenproof frypan.

Top with sliced apples.

Cover and simmer for 15 minutes, then remove cover and cook 12-15 minutes more, until juices have evaporated and apples are starting to caramelise. Remove from heat.

Cut pastry to fit diameter of frypan. Place on top of apples, allowing edges to fall inside the rim.

Bake at 220°C for 20 minutes until pastry is golden. Place a plate on top of pie and carefully flip tart over onto plate. Serve hot.

Serves 6.

Summer Pudding

This healthy dessert is a favourite that will never date. It needs to be prepared at least 8 hours before serving – overnight is better, because the longer it sits, the better it tastes.

Prep time: 10 minutes + chilling

1kg mixed soft berryfruit, hulled

1 cup castor sugar

8-10 slices stale, toast-cut white bread, crusts removed

GARNISH – whipped cream

Place fruit in a large pot and sprinkle over sugar. Bring to a simmer over a very low heat to dissolve sugar. Remove from heat and cool.

Line bottom and sides of a 2 litre glass bowl or pudding basin with slices of bread to cover completely, cutting bread if necessary to ensure it fits closely together.

Ladle fruit and juice into prepared dish and cover completely with a layer of remaining bread.

Cover with a plate that fits inside the pudding basin and weight it with heavy object. Refrigerate for at least 8 hours or overnight.

Turn out onto a large, flat serving plate and accompany with whipped cream.

Serves 6-8.

Bread and Butter Pudding

Like fashion, food tastes come and go, but the best things never really date. This traditional pudding has made a real comeback of late.

Prep time: 10 minutes + chilling
Cook time: 40 minutes

6 thick slices white bread, crusts removed

butter to spread

2/3 cup sultanas

600ml milk

3 eggs

1 tsp vanilla essence

1/4 cup sugar

OPTIONAL – 1 tsp cinnamon or ground cardamom

Line a 20cm x 10cm metal loaf pan with tinfoil or grease a pyrex loaf pan or casserole dish.

Preheat oven to 180°C.

Spread bread lightly on one side with butter. Cut each slice of bread into 3 fingers.

Arrange bread fingers in pan in layers alternately with sultanas.

Beat together milk, eggs, vanilla and sugar. Pour over bread. Leave to stand for at least 15 minutes to 24 hours in the fridge.

Bake at 180°C for 40 minutes. Serve hot or warm.

Serves 4-6.

French Plum Cake

This great recipe makes two moist fruity dessert cakes.

Prep time: 20 minutes

Cook time: 60-65 minutes

6 to 8 fresh plums or other stonefruit

3 tbsp sugar

300g butter

1$\frac{1}{2}$ cups sugar

3 eggs

finely grated rind of $\frac{1}{2}$ lemon

1 tsp vanilla essence

1 cup milk

3$\frac{1}{2}$ cups high grade flour

1 tsp baking powder

Preheat oven to 180°C.

Slice plums into a basin and sprinkle with 3 tbsp sugar. Toss and leave to sit while preparing cake.

Cream together butter and sugar. Add eggs, lemon rind and vanilla essence. Stir in milk, flour and baking powder.

Divide batter between two springform tins. Arrange plums on top.

Bake at 180°C for 60-65 minutes. The fruit will sink into the cake as it cooks.

SERVE warm with whipped cream. Freeze if not using the same day. Use other fruits as available.

Serves 10-12.

Grilled Bananas with Honey and Rum Cream and Chocolate

Any firm fruits will grill well, especially bananas. Here I have halved them, but they can be grilled whole if preferred – they take a little longer and need to be lightly slashed to prevent skins from bursting.

Prep time: 10 minutes

Cook time: 5-8 minutes

6 firm bananas

100ml cream, chilled

1 tbsp runny honey

1-2 tbsp rum

200g chocolate, melted

Cut bananas lengthwise, leaving skins on.

Place on or under a preheated grill plate and cook for 5-8 minutes until skins blacken and bananas are semi-soft.

Whip cream and fold in honey and rum. Arrange bananas on plates with a dollop of cream. Drizzle melted chocolate over cream.

Serves 6.

Chocolate Cheesecake with Fresh Berry Sauce

"Eat me" is the message from this wicked, rich, baked cheesecake. It's a great recipe that whizzes together in the blender.

Prep time: 10 minutes

Cook time: 2 1/4 hours

500g cream cheese

1 cup sugar

3 eggs

2 tsp vanilla

2 tbsp lemon juice

300g sour cream

**200g dark chocolate, melted in a microwave
   or double boiler**

BERRY SAUCE

**3 cups berryfruit, eg raspberries,
   boysenberries, blueberries**

1/2 cup icing sugar

**GARNISH – whole berries,
   sprigs of angelica, cream**

Preheat oven to 150°C.

Blend cream cheese with sugar in a food processor.

Add other ingredients and blend thoroughly.

Line the base and sides of a 22cm springform cake tin with baking paper.

Pour mixture into prepared tin and bake at 150°C for 1 1/4 hours, then turn off oven and leave with door ajar for 1 hour.

Chill well and remove from tin.

Make berry sauce by placing berries and icing sugar in a food processor. Blend until smooth.

SERVE cheesecake slices with sauce. Garnish with whole berries and a sprig of angelica. If desired, drop small dots of cream into sauce and pull a skewer through sauce to form an attractive pattern. Cheesecake keeps well in refrigerator.

Serves 10-12.

Chocolate

Cheesecake

with Fresh

Berry Sauce

Free-form Filo and Berry Pie

Provided it is fresh, filo is one of the easiest and most satisfying pastries to use, moulding into a myriad of sophisticated forms with very little effort. Individual pies can be made by fitting pastry into large muffin pans.

Prep time: 10 minutes

Cook time: 10-12 minutes + 10 minutes standing

melted butter, to brush

6 sheets filo pastry

1 cup strawberry jam

3 tbsp Grand Marnier or other orange liqueur

3-4 punnets mixed fresh berryfruit, eg raspberries, boysenberries, strawberries

icing sugar to dust

Preheat oven to 190°C.

Brush a 30cm x 24cm sponge-roll tin with melted butter.

Lay 2 sheets of pastry into tin on an angle to cover base and sides so that the pastry hangs over some of the edges. Brush with butter.

Overlap another 2 sheets of pastry on top in a spoke pattern and brush with butter. Repeat so that you have a stack overlapping the edges of the baking tin on all sides.

Bake at 190°C for 10-12 minutes until pastry is light golden. Remove from oven, stand for 10 minutes, then carefully remove pastry shell from tin. Place on a wire rack to cool.

Melt jam and stir in liqueur.

Spread jam over base and scatter over berries.

Dust with icing sugar just before serving.

SERVE with creme fraiche or whipped cream.

Serves 8-10.

Kiwifruit Flan

A precooked pastry shell forms the base for a variety of easy desserts with fresh fruit toppings. An easily prepared cream cheese mix makes a delicious layer between the pastry and fruit.

Prep time: 25 minutes

Cook time: 25 minutes

26cm cooked shortcrust pastry crust (see page 108)

FILLING

250g cream cheese

2 tbsp orange juice

2 tbsp icing sugar

1 tsp vanilla essence

4-5 kiwifruit, peeled and sliced into rounds

GLAZE

1/4 cup apricot jam

Blend cream cheese, orange juice, icing sugar and vanilla and spread over cooked pastry base.

Arrange overlapping slices of kiwifruit on top in a decorative pattern.

Melt the jam and strain through a sieve. Brush over the fruit to glaze.

SERVE in wedges.

Serves 6.

Free-form Filo

and Berry Pie

Fabulous Fool

Chilled, whipped cream folded with pureed raw or cooked fruits makes a wonderful, quick dessert. For best results, choose acidic fruit, such as berries, stonefruits, feijoas or pineapple.

Prep time: 15 minutes

600ml chilled cream

2 cups pureed fruit, raw or cooked

about 1/2 cup icing sugar to taste

1 tsp vanilla essence

1 tbsp lemon juice

OPTIONAL – 2 tbsp liqueur of your choice

Whip cream to soft peaks.

Gently fold in all other ingredients.

Refrigerate covered for up to 8 hours before serving.

Serves 6.

Quick Ice cream Combos

Soften 1 litre ice cream and swirl with either –

- 1 tsp ground *ginger* and 1 pkt gingernuts, soaked in 1/4 cup *sherry* then crumbled
- 150g *glace cherries* pureed with 1/4 cup kirsch or cherry brandy
- 150g chopped white *chocolate* and 150g chopped macadamia nuts

Refreeze before serving.

coffee and cake...

Biscotti

Essentially a twice-baked biscuit, biscotti can be made using a variety of nuts and flavourings. Try other combinations such as hazelnuts and cocoa.

Prep time: 15 minutes

Cook time: 35-40 minutes

4 cups plain flour

3/4 cup castor sugar

pinch salt

1 tsp baking powder

1 tsp rosemary leaves, roughly chopped

finely grated rind of 1 orange

finely grated rind and juice of 1 lemon

OPTIONAL – 1 tsp fennel seeds

4 eggs, lightly beaten

1 tsp vanilla essence

100g almonds, roughly chopped

Preheat oven to 200°C.

Place flour, castor sugar, salt, baking powder, rosemary, citrus rinds and fennel seeds in a cake-mixer bowl or food processor.

Mix well. Add eggs and vanilla essence. Blend to form a dough and then mix in nuts.

Divide into 3 or 4 pieces and roll each piece into a log 3cm wide. Place on greased baking sheets and bake for approximately 25 minutes or until firm in middle. Allow to cool slightly. Using a bread knife, cut diagonally into long cookies about 1cm thick. Return to oven for 10-15 minutes to dry, turning once. Cool on wire racks.

Chocolate Brownies

These yummy brownies can be varied with additions such as peppermint essence, finely grated orange rind, or other nuts such as macadamias, hazelnuts or almonds.

Prep time: 20 minutes

Cook time: 35 minutes

225g butter

200g dark chocolate

2 cups sugar

4 eggs

1 1/4 tsp vanilla essence

1 1/2 cups flour

1/2 cup cocoa, sieved

1 1/2 cups walnuts, roughly chopped

TOPPING

200g melted dark chocolate

Preheat oven to 190°C.

Melt butter and chocolate over a low heat.

Combine melted chocolate with sugar. Add eggs, one at a time, beating well after each addition. Stir in vanilla essence.

Mix in flour, cocoa and walnuts until evenly combined. Pour into a greased 30cm x 24cm baking tin. Bake at 180°C for 35 minutes until set. Cool.

TOPPING – Spread melted chocolate over cooled base.

Makes about 24 slices.

Apricot Coconut Slice

The combination of apricots and coconut in this easy, no-cook slice keeps it from tasting too rich. Other dried fruits can also be used, eg figs or prunes.
Prep time: 20 minutes

100g butter
1/2 x 397g tin condensed milk
375g plain sweet biscuits, crushed to crumbs
150g dried apricots, finely chopped
1 cup coconut
2 tbsp lemon juice

Melt butter and condensed milk. Bring to boil. Simmer for 2 minutes. Remove from heat.

Add crushed biscuits, apricots, coconut and lemon juice. Mix well.

Press into a 30cm x 24cm baking tin. Refrigerate until set, then ice.

ICING – Mix 50g melted butter, 3 tbsp boiling water and 1 tsp lemon juice with 3 1/2 cups icing sugar to a smooth consistency. Spread over base.

Store in a cool place in an airtight container.

Makes about 24 slices.

Chocolate Peppermint Slice

This no-cook slice layers a mint filling, a coconut-chocolate base and a rich, dark chocolate topping.
Prep time: 20 minutes

BASE
100g butter
3/4 cup brown sugar
1/2 x 397g tin sweetened condensed milk
250g plain sweet biscuit crumbs
1 cup coconut
1/4 cup cocoa
1 tsp vanilla essence
FILLING – 2 cups icing sugar, 2-3 tbsp oil, 1/4 tsp peppermint essence
TOPPING – 200g dark chocolate, melted

Melt butter, sugar and condensed milk. Bring to boil and simmer, stirring, for 2 minutes. Remove from heat.

Add biscuit crumbs, coconut, cocoa and vanilla essence. Mix well.

Press into a 30cm x 24cm baking tin. Refrigerate. Top with filling when set.

FILLING – Combine icing sugar and oil in saucepan to make a stiff paste. Stir in peppermint essence.

Stir over a low heat until mixture reaches a spreadable consistency. Spread over base. Refrigerate until set. Spread melted chocolate over filling when set.

Coffee Chat

Just when you'd decided that everything **NICE** is bad for you, coffee turns out to be a good guy. Opinion at the moment puts coffee on the "healthy list" for your heart. And you don't have to head for the nearest cafe to **ENJOY** a good cup of coffee – in fact, you don't even need to own a good coffee maker. The best coffee I have ever tasted was in **COLUMBIA**, it was brewed in an old pot and strained through muslin.

What you must have is good quality coffee, preferably **FRESHLY** roasted beans. Buy them regularly and store in a sealed container in your freezer. **GRIND** them straight off the ice, just before you make your brew – it makes a huge difference to the flavour.

START THE DAY WITH cafe latte – a big bowl half to two-thirds full of boiling hot milk, topped with hot, strong espresso.

Get a midday pick-me-up with a **SHORT BLACK**. Strong espresso with a twist of lemon and a crunchy biscotti for dunking.

Wind down with a **LITTLE LUXURY**. Make a brew of strong coffee and sweeten lightly with sugar. Add one to two tablespoons Drambuie (or other liqueur) – a bit more if you're feeling reckless. Pour the coffee over a scoop of vanilla ice cream (choose a big cup or tall glass) and stir until the ice cream melts. **SWEET DREAMS!**

Nutty Caramel Ginger Slice

Ginger aficionados will enjoy this easy, no-cook slice.
Prep time: 15 minutes

BASE
100g butter
1 cup brown sugar
1/2 x 397g tin sweetened condensed milk
250g plain biscuits, crushed to crumbs
1 1/4 cups coconut
2 tsp ground ginger
CARAMEL
2 tbsp butter
1/2 x 397g tin sweetened condensed milk
2 tbsp brown sugar
1 tbsp golden syrup
TOPPING – 1/4 cup walnuts, roughly chopped

Melt butter, sugar and first half of condensed milk for base. Bring to boil. Simmer, stirring constantly, for 2 minutes. Remove from heat.

Add crushed biscuits, coconut and ginger – mix well. Press into a 30cm x 24cm baking tin.

CARAMEL – Melt butter, condensed milk, brown sugar and golden syrup. Bring to boil and simmer for 2 minutes, stirring constantly.

Spread hot caramel over biscuit base. Scatter walnuts over caramel, pressing them into mixture. Refrigerate until set.

Makes about 24 slices.

Chocolate

Brownie

Page 100

Almost Fudgy Choc Cake

If you love chocolate cake, then you'll probably eat all of this rich, moist and almost fudgy cake.

Prep time: 15 minutes
Cook time: 1 hour

100g dark chocolate
100g butter
1/4 cup strong brewed coffee
3 eggs
3/4 cup sugar
1 tsp vanilla essence
2/3 cup flour
1/2 cup raisins
1 cup chopped dark chocolate
Icing sugar to dust

Preheat oven to 180°C.

Melt dark chocolate and butter with coffee over gentle heat until melted, but not too hot.

Beat or blend eggs and sugar together until thick, foamy and pale yellow – about 5-7 minutes. Add vanilla. Gradually beat in chocolate mixture.

Fold in flour, then add raisins and chocolate chips.

Pour mixture into a greased 20cm cake tin and bake at 180°C for about 1 hour. Cool in tin, then turn onto a serving platter and dust with icing sugar.

Serves 6-8.

Coconut and Feijoa Cake

Tangy pieces of fruit contrast with the rich, tropical flavour of coconut in this wonderful cake.

Prep time: 15 minutes
Cook time: 1 hour 10 minutes

150g butter
1 1/2 cups castor sugar
4 eggs, separated
2 cups coconut
2 cups self-raising flour
1 tsp baking powder
1 cup milk
pinch of salt
1 cup peeled chopped feijoas, or other acid
   fruit, eg plums, blueberries
icing sugar to dust

Preheat oven to 150°C.

Beat butter and sugar until light and fluffy.

Add egg yolks, one at a time, beating well after each addition.

Fold coconut and sifted flour and baking powder into butter and egg mixture. Fold in milk.

Beat egg whites and salt to form soft peaks. Gently fold into mixture with fruit.

Line a 23cm cake tin with baking paper. Spoon cake mixture into tin, smoothing the top.

Bake at 150°C for 1 hour and 10 minutes. Cool in the tin. Sprinkle with icing sugar if desired.

Serves 8-10.

Chocolate Chip Pound Cake

Ricotta cheese adds lightness and improves the keeping qualities of this moist cake. Cottage cheese can also be used if it is pureed or sieved.

Prep time: 15 minutes

Cook time: 1 hour

150g butter, softened

250g ricotta or pureed cottage cheese

1 cup sugar

3 eggs

1 tsp vanilla essence

finely grated rind of $1/2$ orange

2 cups flour

2 tsp baking powder

$1/4$ cup milk combined with $1/2$ tsp baking soda

$3/4$ cup chopped dark chocolate chips

Chocolate

Chip Pound

Cake

Preheat oven to 160°C. Grease and line a 20cm cake tin.

Beat butter, ricotta and sugar until light and fluffy.

Beat in eggs, one at a time. Add vanilla essence and rind.

Combine flour and baking powder. Stir into creamed mixture, with milk and chocolate chips, until evenly combined.

Spoon batter into tin, smoothing top.

Bake at 160°C for 1 hour or until a skewer inserted in the centre comes out clean.

Ice with orange frosting when cold (see Springtime Orange Cake, page 106, for recipe).

Serves 8-12.

Springtime Orange Cake

Melt-in-the-mouth moist and tender, this simple cake is a good tin filler.

Prep time: 20 minutes

Cook time: 1 hour 25 minutes

200g butter

2 cups sugar

4 eggs, lightly beaten

1 $\frac{1}{2}$ tsp vanilla essence

4 cups flour

1 tbsp baking powder

1 $\frac{1}{2}$ cups milk

finely grated rind of 1 orange

ORANGE FROSTING

125g cream cheese

2 cups icing sugar

2 tsp orange juice

Optional – finely grated rind of $\frac{1}{2}$ orange

Beat together butter and sugar until creamy. Gradually add beaten eggs, mixing until well combined. Add vanilla essence.

Add dry ingredients and milk, together with the grated rind. Pour into a greased 23cm spring-form tin. Bake at 180°C for 1 hour 25 minutes until skewer comes out clean.

FROSTING – soften cream cheese and mix in remaining ingredients. Stir until creamy. Cover top and sides of cake.

Ginger and Pineapple Upside-Down Cake

Whizzed together in a blender, this easy cake is light, and moist, and also makes a great pudding. Chopped walnuts can be used in place of glace ginger if preferred.

Prep time: 15 minutes

Cook time: 45 minutes

2 cups self-raising flour

1 tsp baking soda

finely grated rind of 1 orange

2 eggs

1 cup milk

$\frac{3}{4}$ cup brown sugar

$\frac{1}{3}$ cup golden syrup

$\frac{1}{2}$ cup salad oil

1 tsp ground ginger

TOPPING

50g butter, melted

$\frac{1}{2}$ cup brown sugar

2 tbsp golden syrup

225g can pineapple rings, drained

$\frac{1}{2}$ cup chopped glace ginger

Preheat oven to 180°C.

Place all ingredients for cake batter in a blender or mixer bowl and quickly process until smooth.

Melt topping butter with sugar and golden syrup. Spread over the base of a 23cm loose-bottomed cake tin.

Arrange pineapple and ginger over sugar. Pour over batter. Bake at 180°C for 45 minutes.

Ginger and

Pineapple

Upside-Down

Cake

Here's How...

Pre-cooked Pastry Shell

Roll pastry out to cover base and sides of a pie or flan dish. Chill for 15 minutes. Preheat oven to 200°C.

Cut a round of greaseproof paper to fit base of dish. Place dried beans or baking blind material on top to weigh down.

Bake for 15 minutes, remove beans and paper and bake for a further 10 minutes until pastry is crisp and golden.

Cheat's Hollandaise

Blend or beat together 2 eggs, a pinch of salt and the juice of $1/2$ lemon.

Heat 100g butter until boiling and pour this in a slow stream into the mixture, beat or blend all the time until fully absorbed. The sauce will thicken on cooling.

Makes $3/4$ cup. Reheat with care, as sauce will curdle if overheated.

Cream Cheese Icing

Soften 125g cream cheese. Mix in 2 cups icing sugar, finely grated rind of $1/2$ lemon and 2 tsp lemon juice.

Beat until smooth.

Croutons with French Bread

Cut french bread into 1cm-thick diagonal slices. Brush both sides of bread with olive oil.

Bake at 180°C for 15-20 minutes, until golden in colour.

How to Melt Chocolate

Place roughly chopped chocolate in top of double saucepan or in metal bowl over a saucepan of near boiling water.

Stir until chocolate melts and is smooth.

To microwave – place roughly chopped chocolate in a microwave proof dish.

Cook on 100% power, stirring every 30 seconds until almost dissolved. Remove and stir well until completely melted.

Mayonnaise

Blend together 2 tsp dry mustard, 1 tsp salt, $1/2$ tsp white pepper, 1 tsp sugar, $1/4$ cup lemon juice, $1/2$ tsp finely grated lemon rind and 3-4 egg yolks.

With motor running, add about $2^{1/2}$ cups salad oil slowly in a thin continuous stream until it is fully incorporated and the mayonnaise is very thick.

Keep refrigerated. Makes $2^{1/2}$ cups.

(See page 30 for flavour variations).

Lemons Pickled in Oil

Cut 6 lemons into thin wedges. Freeze until firm. Sprinkle over 6 tbsp coarse salt, and leave for about an hour.

Layer the slices into sterilised jars and pour on any brine that has collected on the plate. Sprinkle paprika between the layers, and tuck a bay-leaf in the top. Cover with corn or soya oil.

Uses – the liquid is good as an alternative to vinegar or fresh lemon juice in dressing. To use lemons, discard pulp and slice rinds finely. Add to salads, fish, chicken or vegetable dishes. A great condiment for grills and barbecues.

Poaching an Egg

Using a frypan, fill it with water to a level of 5cm. **Bring** to boil. Break egg into water. Reduce heat to a light simmer and poach eggs for 3-4 minutes.

A little vinegar added to the water will seal the egg white.

Roasting Peppers

Preheat a grill. Place red, green or yellow peppers on a baking tray and grill until skin blackens and blisters, turning regularly. When skin is blistered, remove from oven, cool, then peel off skins and remove white tissue and seeds.

Separating Eggs

Crack egg by tapping shell with a knife. Tip yolk from one half of shell to the other, allowing the white to fall into a bowl.

To Peel and Segment an Orange

Cut thin slice off one end of orange.

Place cut-side down on a flat surface and, using a sawing action, cut peel and pith off in strips. Remove any remaining pith.

To segment, run a sharp knife close to the membranes, cutting through to the centre, to release each segment.

Vinaigrette Dressing

Combine the following ingredients in a jar: 3 tbsp spiced vinegar or lemon juice or balsamic vinegar or wine vinegar, $1/2$ cup extra virgin olive oil, $1/2$ tsp each mustard and sugar, and salt and pepper to season.

Place lid on jar and shake well. Store in refrigerator.

Your food looks even better when presented on a range of exciting tableware. There's no need to use a complete dinner set. Buy unusual, individual pieces to add drama to your table. We are very grateful to a number of our friends and local specialist tableware shops for providing us with wonderful serving plates and dishes.

Catherine Anselmi, Newmarket
Fables, Newmarket
Corso di Fiori, Newmarket
Living and Giving, Newmarket
Askew, Parnell
The Store, Newmarket
Sasak Pottery, The House Company